T0315194

Praise for

Pop Magick

"Alex Kazemi has his finger on the pulse of magick and all its wonders."
—GEORGE NOORY, Host of *Coast to Coast AM*

"We live in dangerous times. We are all subject to unseen forces—social, technological, biological—that have programmed and conditioned us, like Pavlov's dogs, to behave without thinking. The way out of this maze is difficult. *Pop Magick* is an exciting and unconventional attempt to help us all deprogram, through methods culled from primal sources in magic and alchemy. This in the tradition of people like Gurdjieff and Colin Wilson, the tradition of trying to wake us up from our slumber. You have nothing to lose but your chains." —ROBERT GREENE

"Alex Kazemi is a boy wonder." —SHIRLEY MANSON

"My favorite millennial provocateur." —BRET EASTON ELLIS

"I want to heal. This book should help me along my treacherous path to better understanding myself." —BELLA THORNE

"Can a small step change your life? Of course it can. Alex Kazemi provides a treasure map of simple yet revolutionary possibilities which, if practiced with passion, can lead you to magick, self-discovery, and more rabbit holes than you can dive into."
—MITCH HOROWITZ, PEN Award-winning author of *Occult America* and *The Miracle Club*

"This book will help you discover tools that expand your consciousness and manifest your deepest desires. I'm happy to see that Transcendental Meditation is part of Alex's journey to find strength in the stillness within." —BOB ROTH, author of *Strength in Stillness*

"A modern, hip, no-nonsense approach to magick rooted in consciousness, and changing the self, and the world, for the better. Practical and esoteric, serious and funny, *Pop Magick* is an alchemical paradox designed to show you a new way of seeing and being in the world that will defy ordinary expectations."

—CHRISTOPHER PENCZAK, Author and Co-Founder of the Temple of Witchcraft

"There was Bob Dylan and his surrealist voice under helium back in 1965, you will soon have Alex Kazemi and his poetic visions intravenously…"

—MIRWAIS

"*Pop Magick* is edgy, transparent, and empowering. It's a real world look at how to start breaking out of the 'Matrix,' or as Alex Kazemi calls it, 'The Simulation.' It's how real magick can be used for good in our lives today, and in service to others' lives who we touch. It's a beginner's guidebook on how to get started with living a more magical life. It's written in a very hip and fun way that directly addresses social trends in the 21st century, by a millennial for millennials on how to be an influencer in today's counter-culture and pop culture, to help steer the course of creating a better world."

—DR. THERESA BULLARD, Host of *Mystery Teachings* on Gaia TV and Modern Mystery School Teacher

Pop Magick

Pop Magick

A Simple Guide to Bending Your Reality

Alex Kazemi

PERMUTED
PRESS

A PERMUTED PRESS BOOK

Pop Magick:
A Simple Guide to Bending Your Reality
© 2020 by Alex Kazemi
All Rights Reserved

ISBN: 978-1-68261-880-6
ISBN (eBook): 978-1-68261-881-3

Cover art by JS Aurelius
Author photo by Conor Cunningham

PERMUTED
PRESS
Permuted Press, LLC
New York • Nashville
permutedpress.com

Published in the United States of America

*To anyone who has ever felt
like they don't belong in this world.*

TABLE OF CONTENTS

FOREWORD

Magick is the art of utilizing natural forces around us to bring about change. I stand for change. That's what this book does. It brings change—change of thought, change of action, change of spirit.

Magick is neutral—neither good nor evil. Take this book for what it is: a look behind and beyond the mirror. Come on the journey.

—*Rose McGowan*

INTRODUCTION

Welcome to a new magickal age. The age of pop magick.

If you are ready to learn how to bend yourself and bend reality through the practical applications of magick, then it's time for you to get weird and dive deep into the infinite otherworld.

Pop magick is magick for us, the people. It's not something to be kept secret. Pop magick is for those who feel we are all magickal beings currently navigating the human experience. Deep down in our souls we know there is more than what we have been taught by society, that the mystical forces around us are filled with purpose and possibility. Pop magick is for anyone who wants to engage those energies moving through the astral plane and collaborate with them in our own journeys through this temporal existence.

Magick is not about adhering to dogma or defining yourself through aesthetics or binaries. It's about doing and practicing. It's about action. It's about performing ritual experiments and producing results. It's about recharging and expanding your freedom. It's about exploration and discovery. It's about knowing you have the power to change yourself and to change reality, to influence events by channeling the energies inside of you outward, with intention. Practicing magick is all about your natural ability to access your will to bring order to chaos. The more results you produce, the more you will find yourself living a magickal life.

Magick becomes what you choose to make of it by inviting it into your life. When you open yourself up to magick you are opening yourself up to the universe and its limitless potential to impact your life in ways that are substantive and positive.

Magick is within your grasp, available to access right now. All it takes is your will and commitment. There is no right or wrong way to do magick, no good or bad way to practice it. You are the one who builds your bridge to the astral plane, establishing your own rules and guidelines along the way. The process of discovering your true self and divine will begins and ends with you.

Magick is a means to improve yourself and your life, whether it's helping you survive the onslaught of the daily grind by bringing you peace and joy or helping you achieve your goals by providing you with discipline and focus. Magick is a partner you can lean on to help you build the life you truly want to live.

Are you ready to dip your toes into celestial pools? Do you want to feel a full moon lunar rush? It's time to access the inner treasure chest of tools and tap into the energies humming in the otherworlds to bend reality and change your life.

1

MAGICK

I've never believed that you could simply wish upon a lucky star to get what you want. I believed you had to create the things that you want to see in the world yourself. People always ask me, "Why do you have so many of the things you want? How are you living your dream life?" My answer is always the same: magick.

Magick is an inherent spiritual system that I didn't know I had within me. Maybe you don't realize this either. Hardly any of us do. We have to use our will to access it. Once we do, we are never the same again.

Magick is how I live in a world where angels communicate with me through repeating numbers. I get to infect pop viruses into our culture, and my emotions are alchemized from reactive states into fuel used to propel me towards my goals. Magick is also how I can access a fountain of internal peace within.

Magick has taken me, a dude from the suburbs of Vancouver, Canada, everywhere from hanging out with the man who taught Oprah meditation to Marilyn Manson tweeting about my art to some of the most secret behind-the-scenes parties in Hollywood. But the most important thing I've received is the VIP pass to the angelic space within that I needed to reach the divine will and the power to transform from an automatic-traumatized-outsider-addict boy into a connected, recovered young man.

What you've heard is true. Magick has led to a collaboration with Selena Gomez and Petra Collins on a piece for *Dazed*, a conversation with Taylor Swift, a dinner in Beverly Hills with *American Psycho* author Bret Easton Ellis, becoming pen pals with Camille Paglia, and Madonna publicly expressing excitement on Instagram about an image that wouldn't exist had I not willed it into existence. In under five years of practicing magick, I have connected myself to some of the most iconic people our world has ever seen, and almost all of my living heroes. Now I'm going to teach you how—with divine will—to access, remix, and take back your life from the magickal-energy suck world of today. Are you ready for pop magick, baby?

In pop magick, magick has two definitions:

1. Magick is the science, art, and practice of bending reality in accordance with your true will.
2. Magick is the science, art, and practice of accessing your divine will to bring order to chaos.

Magick is a technology to focus, direct, and communicate our will to the natural universe to bend reality, affect changes, and produce results in the material world. The practice of magick is all about tapping into the unlimited resource of natural energy within yourself. You are the cause of your effect. It's about taking chances and trying different variables to produce either specific or abstract outcomes. It's about taking back your power and developing an awareness that you have the ability to direct your energy. You are sending your will to the unseen worlds by alchemizing it into energy.

Something you must accept now before you begin practicing this science is that all of magick is theory. There is no evidence as to why it works. You, as the practitioner, will stitch together your own theories through your original data, i.e. your lived evidence accumulated from your own practice and experience. Mystery is what makes practicing magick so powerful.

Why dismiss something as fiction just because we don't understand it? Magick is not an act of the supernatural. Though it can sometimes seem nonsensical, and it operates on its own set of rules and logic—also known as total fucking chaos—it is of the natural world. No one can give you magickal power. You have to do the work to earn it.

Magick is not instantaneous, and there is no magic-bullet method to materialize something into the physical world. All we know is that through a practitioner's transmission, magick can cause change in the physical world.

Some magickal practitioners believe that almost anything you do with will or intention is a magickal act. Something as simple as buying a Pepsi from 7-Eleven, by classic occult-definitions, can be a magickal act. You set your intention and will and achieved a result.

Magickal practitioners who receive results always think of things that can happen in the material world. There are no limits to the beliefs, but there is logic. Asking to grow angel wings or to wake up with six-pack abs is science fiction. However, you can perform a spell to seek the discipline to go to the gym and then create momentum in the material world that could result in the achievement of a muscular stomach.

No one knows how magick works. We simply know that it does. I'm sure most of us can't explain how a phone charger cord works to charge our iPhones, but we still do it every day. Sometimes you don't need to know how something works. When we practice magick, we plug into the unknown energies that are zipping and zapping around us.

Magick does not require belief to work, but I do think believing in magick, and having a will to discover it through your concrete sense of knowing, is how you can discover it in all areas of your life, including your practice. Even if you choose to not believe in its existence, magick is always happening because practitioners are experiencing results.

You, the practitioner, are the one who gets to define whether magick is something that you do, or if magick is something you were born to be.

Remember: There is no such thing as coincidence, only magick.

2

MAGICKAL RITUAL

Have you ever prayed? If so, you have participated in a magickal ritual. You have successfully interacted, bridged, and acknowledged the unseen dimensions whether you refer to this union as the astral plane, spirit world, or the kingdom of heaven. You have requested the materialization of something to be sent to you from beyond this physical world. The only difference between a prayer and a ritual is that prayer relies on surrender, and magick requires you to tap into the energy within to create the outcome you seek. A magickal ritual uses the combination of props, timing, visualization, and directing your will to release the energy to create a change in the material world.

In the context of witchcraft, a magickal ritual is a spell. A spell is simply directing your energy to a prop with the intention of producing an outcome. All of us witches, sorcerers, and magickal practitioners are playing with the same unknown forces right under the same blue skies as our ancestors. We don't give a fuck that we cannot fully comprehend or understand magick. We just know that it exists and works. You must take responsibility when making the decision to bring order to any chaos that is caused by a magickal ritual. It is *your* energy being sent out, after all. Go into ritual work with curiosity, openness, and a belief in all possibilities. Don't let your prejudices or preconceptions keep you stuck in a lower version of reality.

THE INGREDIENTS USED IN THE PERFORMANCE OF A POP MAGICK RITUAL

Intention + Desire + Will

How do you decide on your intention? It's simple. Ask yourself what you want. What is the reason you are doing this spell? What is the outcome you desire? If you could light a candle and, by the end of it, effect nature's order to bring something about, what would it be? Do you even know why you want it? When you identify your will, you are allowing your conscious self to take charge of your subconscious self. Try to challenge your own will. What do you dream of experiencing, and what do you believe you are capable of? Challenge yourself by asking: "Is this coming from the pools of my soul, the essence of my true self?"

Timing

In pop magick, the moon is our clock. We tune ourselves to be conscious of nature's rhythms to create the most effective results in our practice. During the light of the moon, the two weeks following the new moon (when the moon is waxing), we perform rituals to draw things into our lives. During the dark of the moon, the two weeks after the full moon (when the moon is waning), we perform rituals to alchemize what no longer serves us. On the full moon, we are at our most powerful, and so is our magick. Any type of ritual is more likely to succeed when done under a full moon. On the new moon, we perform rituals revolving around new beginnings and spiritual rebirth after surviving the trials of the waning moon.

Props

In pop magick, there is no paraphernalia or prop that has inherent magickal power. You can use anything in a ritual. You are the power. Candles, sigils, poppets, and ribbons—common essential ritual ingredients—are not inherently powerful, but when you bring them into ritual and charge them with your energy, they become powerful tools and factors in achieving results. Some practitioners swear by using green candles for success spells, but what if you want to use a red one? Gasp! What if you achieve a result for a success spell using a red one? Do what you want by trusting your soul's compass. There are no right or wrong rules. I swear the only reason I met Taylor Swift was because I did spells at my friend's house using tap water from his kitchen sink. Was the tap water magickal? Nah. Sometimes there are magickal emergencies. One time, I stopped and did a spell with a tree on a sidewalk in the middle of the day for my phone's keyboard (I use a burner phone) to get fixed. It worked. Thanks, sidewalk tree.

Raising the Energy

Raising the energy is your magickal pregame. It's like getting your-self as psyched up as possible before you are going somewhere, but, in this case, you are going to your ritual. Do whatever gets you in the mood for a big night out or a celebration. You want to put your energy on full blast and blow out the speakers. It is advised to raise the energy before every magickal ritual. Emotion is your aid. You want to achieve a level of potency, increasing your vibe to the highest degree possible, to the point where your whole body is buzzing. This will increase the likelihood of achieving a result.

Your highly charged feelings and thoughts of why you feel so strongly about what it is you want will amp you up to direct and release the energy of your will. Sometimes I want something so badly I don't need to raise the vibe because I am in such a highly charged emotional state, and I am desperate to release the excitement over what I want. On a full moon, though, I religiously dance to "Hands to Myself" by Selena Gomez. I bang my body in the air, spin in circles, and close my eyes. I totally lose myself and enter a trance state. Do whatever builds the power up in your body. Do anything that builds emotion for you. Try to chant while you dance, so you can feel the buildup of energy.

In pop magick, this is how we alter our state of consciousness, by dancing to pop music under full moons. Crazy, right? You can use dancing, trance, any type of music, colors, and symbols to alter your state. Anything that compels you to feel magickal and to enter a zero-mind state. I don't condone staying up for days, using drugs as a means of a portal to access powerful entities, or forcing yourself into dangerous situations to alter your state of conscious-ness. Some magickal practitioners swear by these experiments to "open up the gates to the otherworlds." If that's the way you roll, go for it, and tell me how it works out for you. I've been getting prime results with my Gomez gate-to-the-other-worlds regime.

Visualization

This either might disappoint you or make you super stoked, but the same kind of visualization that Oprah talks about is the exact same technique that witches, occultists, and magickal practitioners have always used to cast out and charge the energy for a specific outcome via ritual or spells. (Cue cultural appropriation occult versus new age debate here!)

At this very moment, can you picture in your mind the last website you visited? The outside of the last shop you went into? Your favorite pair of shoes? Your favorite Disney character? This is visualization: the conscious decision to see with your mind as opposed to your eyes. In a magickal ritual, we create in our mind images that do not yet exist. Visualization is conscious lucid dreaming, holding a will to activate that place where it all feels so real. You are catapulting something, setting magick into motion, sending out and releasing your energies to bring forth something into our material world.

The only difference in pop magick is we are conscious of the variables and factors. We believe in the moon's influence on our energy and will. We are scientists of this technique who are constantly testing out different ways to achieve results. It all comes back to this. Magickal practitioners don't believe in thinking positive and doing nothing. Pop magick is about creating results in the real world.

Direction + Release of the Energy

1. Close your eyes and imagine what it would be like to have what it is that you want. Imagine the feeling it would give you right now.

2. See yourself as if you are there inside of the end result you are putting your will towards. Think of the sounds you would hear, what you would see, and what it would look like. Do everything you can to paint the most graphic visual in your mind of what it would be like to have what it is that you want. Imagine the exact feeling of experiencing the end result as if it is happening right now.

3. Feel the energy beaming from your body. Feel all the euphoria casting out of you. Think of putting all of yourself and all of your will directed at this exact result. Think of how this desire is coming from the highest most authentic streams of your soul. Try to think of how, at some point, you wanted something so badly you literally felt like you would die if you didn't have it. Experience those graphic feelings of passion, desire, and the will to get it. Involve and immerse yourself in this need, and validate that this need is real for you. Now direct that passion, desire, and will towards that end result bursting in your mind. When you feel you can no longer hold the energy inside, release it. Let it all out. The magick begins once you expel the energy. You will know when you are ready to release. When you feel you cannot hold the energy anymore, release the energy! The magick has begun.

4. Forget about the magick. Forget about the results. Let it go, and let it work.

3

HOW TO MATERIALIZE MAGICKAL ENERGY

Rub your palms together for twenty-two seconds. Start slow but then rub faster and faster. Feel your muscles tense up. Let your palms grow hot. Stop and hold your palms about three inches apart from each other. Can you feel them tingle? This is a materialization of magickal energy.

When you rub your palms together and use the rest of your body to raise the energy, that is generating magickal energy.

Start to recognize this energy as the same type of feelings that arise from our body when we are horny, terrified, angry, nervous, or euphoric. In pop magick, emotion = energy! Energy can be molded like a metaphysical snowball.

You hold the ability to alchemize and release the magickal energy from within you. Raise, control, and direct!

4

SPECIFIC OUTCOME AND ABSTRACT OUTCOME MAGICK

In pop magick, there are two types of magick:

1. **SOM:** Specific outcome magick is the intention to materialize a specific outcome into the material world.
2. **AOM:** Abstract outcome magick is the intention to materialize an abstract outcome into the material world.

Specific outcome magick is when we cast out our energies to create a specific outcome in our reality. A specific outcome can be anything: the exact job that you want, the exact romantic partner you want, the exact sexual partner you want, the exact text message you want to receive. This is the most common form of magick and the reason most magickal practitioners perform rituals.

In my earlier magickal days, I did SOM almost every day. I couldn't stop once I realized that the more I practiced SOM rituals, the more the things I wanted actually happened.

I have received life-changing results practicing SOM, but I have also received devastating results. I have gotten the things I wanted and then felt empty, ashamed, and depressed after because of the amount of chaos caused and the people who got hurt in the long run. I have hurt myself a lot doing SOM. I had fallen far past being seduced by the illusion of the material world. I am not reducing SOM to selfish or narcissistic behaviors, but I will say it's easy to become greedy. You might learn at some point on your path that surrendering to the natural order of events, allowing life to happen, and handing over your trust to the spirit guides can create beautiful, specific outcomes. You might switch between SOM or AOM. I would be lying if I didn't credit SOM to an acceleration in my career success. I would be lying if I said SOM wasn't the reason you are holding this book in your hands.

What I learned practicing SOM is that the material things I accrued through ritual were never going to make me happy, and the good things I received through ritual that were spiritually nourishing likely would have happened anyway.

A lot of magickal practitioners are fully dedicated to the belief that nothing can be manifested unless you manifest it on the astral plane first, but I challenge that belief by my lived experience. I have attained things I've wanted and needed without doing SOM.

What I have learned from practicing magick is that the events that need to happen in your life will happen.

Abstract outcome magick is when you cast out your energies to bring something into your life without having a specific outcome in mind. An abstract outcome could be asking for more joy or asking for a job opportunity that will make you happy even though you have no idea what that job might be. AOM is about not knowing how to get something but believing it is possible to receive it without knowing the practical plan to achieve it. You are trusting the universe to send you trials and symbols to bend reality. AOM is similar to prayer or sending out a "wish" without specific clarity, something that is a charm and won't harm anyone. You can go as far as using universal energy instead of your own and just trying to be a vessel to send out the higher energies to influence a positive outcome.

AOM could be viewed as clean or cautious magick. From my own experience, when I have done AOM there has been little to no chaos when the results manifest. It seems harmonious—events aligning to a point of perfection. It feels like a dream, something that was always meant to happen. I feel AOM is happening on those flow days where things just feel good and right. AOM is the kind of magick that happens in life when you don't expect it and didn't think you would receive it.

5

WHERE TO APPLY MAGICK

Are you ready to obtain that job you've always wanted? Do you want to love yourself in ways you never believed possible? Do you want to be more driven and disciplined, achieving the goals you fantasize about? There are rituals for each of these things and more!

Magick can be employed in all areas of your life to create opportunities. I have used magick to collaborate with my icons, to help people, and to completely restructure my way of being. I've become friends with people who I seem to have known in a past life because of our spiritual connection. I've extracted myself from complicated demonic trials. I've alchemized destructive states into willpower. I have used magick to positively influence the lives of others—with their permission of course.

Magick is something I use every day, and can do it anywhere.

Prior to practicing magick, I didn't know how to utilize the energy of desire and will. I would let it completely take me over, but now I can alchemize and redirect that passion towards ritual while taking practical steps toward realizing my goal.

I may have done rituals on multiple moon phases to materialize the book you are holding, but it didn't arrive out of thin air. It still required a dedicated work ethic and divine will. The combination of hard work and the power of nature is how I achieve successful results in my daily life.

AREAS IN WHICH TO APPLY MAGICK

- Self-love
- Self-improvement
- Career
- Purpose
- Alchemy
- Protection
- Sex/love/romance
- Helping others

And anything else you can think of that is of the natural world.

Remember: there are no specific or correct correspondences when doing a ritual. It's all about what feels right for you as the practitioner and what you associate with the area of life you are deciding to work on. I can do a self-love spell with a rock I find on the ground, and it could be just as effective as using a pink candle that corresponds with Libra. There are no rules, only magick.

Before doing a ritual, ask yourself: "What do I want?" See if it feels right—whether it's coming from your soul. Try to understand *why* you desire the result that you want before doing magick. Your intention should be meaningful and genuine.

6

TYPES OF SPELLS
OR RITUALS

The concept of performing a magickal ritual can be all kinds of intimidating at first. Most people panic: "Am I doing this right? Did I buy the right kind of candle? Do I have to buy fifty-dollar oils online that some witch in Salem made in order for my spell to work? Do I have to read 300 books on the occult to master the correct technique of practicing a magickal ritual?"

This is nonsense. Magick can be done anywhere at any time. Anything can become magickal and used as a ritual tool. Magick comes from accessing and using your free will to wield the power within you. Whatever you choose to use in a ritual is functioning as a prop that *you* charge with your energy. The real magick is happening from your will, your intention, the pictures in your mind of what you would like to see in your reality.

The first spell I did was with nail polish remover I found in my sister's bathroom, and it worked great. In emergencies, I have used trees, water, and spit. The visual representation of a spell or ritual can greatly help remind your subconscious mind that this is energy that needs to be externalized in order to achieve the results you want.

I do believe the collective consciousness has put so much emphasis towards certain magickal tools being inherently powerful. A belief that a candle is powerful could *possibly* bring more results out of a ritual, but nothing is fixed as fact. The magickal practitioners who wear robes with Aleister Crowley symbols on them in some coven are not practicing any more powerful magick than you can, at home, in your pjs on a Monday night.

In pop magick, there are four beginner-pack magickal devices to choose from to get you started: candle magick, sigil magick, elemental magick, and sex magick.

Try to listen to the compass that is your soul. You have to do what feels right for you. I've tried sigil magick, but I prefer candle magick. I think sigil magick is powerful, and I like to use it to charge symbols or create art that I hope will have a mass audience. I cast it out with the intention I want people to feel when they look at the work.

It's your choice to do what you want.

Remember: No rules, only theory!

7

CANDLE MAGICK

If you've ever blown out birthday candles on a cake after making a wish, you've performed candle magick. You set out your intention and wished to bring something out of the unknown and into the material world while charging a prop (the birthday candle) with your magickal energy.

Staring at a flickering candle can transport you out of the mundanity of everyday reality and into a dream state, moving you from this world into unseen worlds. If not for candle magick, you wouldn't be reading this book. Candle magick is something I do almost every day. It's been the most fun and successful form of magick for me and has done everything from advancing my career to healing me during times of emotional pain to bringing me out of unthinkable darkness. I always like to say to young witches, "It takes just one candle to change your life!" More on this at the end of the chapter.

Candles are cinematic and haunting. Because of that, candle magick is my personal favorite. I love stocking up on oil-blends and little candles at the local metaphysical store or finding them when I travel to different cities to bring back home for my practice. Using essential oils in candle magick rituals is a great way to build the psychic link with the candle. You don't need a special moon-charged oil off of Etsy. You can use any type of oil and make your own blends. Or you can pick up blends from local stores. It's cool to interact with the like-minded energies around and support other magick practitioners.

The oils we use in candle magick can create powerful links and associations with the life energy of flowers and herbs. As a practitioner of magick, it can be powerful to create conscious associations and links with your will. Whenever I practice candle magick, I can feel myself awakening the inner witch within me.

When I am alone with a candle, I access the divine part of myself that disappears from society on the night of a full moon and runs into the woods to surrender to the lunar power. Practicing candle magick is a sacred ritual for me because it creates a sensual sensory experience and connects me to the inner gratitude I have to be using my will to create a magickal life for myself. I am reminded of the wonderment of life. Sometimes when I do candle magick, as I'm rubbing the candle, it feels like my fingers are chanting to open up the gates of the astral world. I love the burning crackle when my spit hits the flame.

Candles themselves are not powerful. Only when you charge candles with your fingers and seal them with your energy do they become magickal. Some witches don't even touch the candles. They just ask for an abstract outcome to materialize or come forward in their lives. You have to figure out how to connect to the divine in a way that feels the most powerful for you. You decide how you put the energy into the candle.

Ending a candle magick spell can vary. Some people leave the candle to burn out on its own, believing it is being released into the infinite cosmos. Some people snuff the flame, while others blow it out. I blow out the candle to symbolically release the magick and close the spell. Sometimes in ritual, the flame will extinguish itself on its own, and some magickal practitioners believe that means the spell is over.

No matter how you close your candle spell, your intention will spread and evaporate into the ether. So mote it be!

HOW TO DO CANDLE MAGICK

1. Choose a candle.
2. Pour an essential oil onto your fingertips and dress the candle with it (or with your own spit) to seal it with magickal energy.
3. Close your eyes and rub your fingertips up and down the candle as you infuse and charge the prop with your intention. Feel the magick energy from your fingertips being released into the candle, building a psychic link from your mind to the physical plane.
4. Once you are ready to burst, direct the magick toward your intention. If you feel called to, blow the candle out or snuff it to symbolize the end of the ritual and release the energy.

WHAT COLOR CANDLE SHOULD I USE?

There are no rules. It's up to you and your intuition. It would be impossible to say what one color means, because all perceptions are subjective. The symbolic meaning and how a color affects you psychologically and emotionally is up to you. Every color in the spectrum carries a special vibe, but that vibe can only be determined by you. The vibe coming from the color of the candle is personal.

Magickal symbols and correspondences all depend on the wielder—the person engaging with the prop. To one person, a black candle might be success and love, while to another person a red candle might be healing and purification. There is no right or wrong association. You have to define these things yourself. You will create your own template and set of rules for how you want to develop your candle magick practice.

The following list of traditional color correspondences is something you should question, remix, and redefine to find what works best for your soul.

Colors of Candle Magick

Red represents love, urgency, passion, and summoning.

- Magickal workings include enhancing romance, enhancing sexual passion, converting sexual energy into motivation, and speeding things up.
- Element: Fire
- Sign: Aries

Green represents health, growth, money, and the material plane.

- Magickal workings include enhancing job opportunities for financial gain, starting a health regimen, bringing forward results, and materializing goals.
- Element: Earth
- Sign: Taurus

Yellow represents communication, intellect, intelligence, and happiness.

- Magickal workings include improving social skills, strengthening status, bringing forward mental clarity, strengthening brain power, and travel.
- Element: Air
- Sign: Gemini

Silver represents magick, alchemy, receptivity, and secrets.

- Magickal workings include enhancing synchronicity in your life, finding magick within yourself, bringing forward wonder, and all forms of alchemy.
- Sign: Cancer

Gold represents fame, status, power, and attention.

- Magickal workings include enhancing fame, meeting successful people, bringing forward productivity, and finding success.
- Sign: Leo

White represents healing, purification, cleanliness, and light.

- Magickal workings include enhancing inner-truth, bathing yourself in light, bringing forward innocence, and achieving purification.
- Sign: Virgo

Pink represents friendship, harmony, self-love, and the divine femme.

- Magickal workings include enhancing self-love, seeing inner and external beauty, bringing forward duality, and enhanced senses.
- Sign: Libra

Blue represents imagination, feelings, emotions, and tranquility.

- Magickal workings include enhancing your empathy for yourself and those around you, starting a meditation habit, bringing forward inner calm, and soothing.
- Element: Water
- Sign: Scorpio

Orange represents willpower, success, optimism, and discipline.

- Magickal workings include new beginnings, stimulating healthy habits, activating motivation, accessing confidence, and strengthening.
- Sign: Sagittarius

Black represents evil, the shadow-self, confusion, and darkness.

- Magickal workings include converting negative energy and self-destructive urges into light, removing negativity, shadow balancing, protection against harm, and getting rid of anything.
- Sign: Capricorn

Grey represents detachment, revolution, rebellion, and independence.

- Magickal workings include enhancing solitary time in your life, breaking rules, bringing forward assertiveness, and encouraging rebelliousness.
- Sign: Aquarius

Purple represents wisdom, psychic abilities, imagination, and the gates to the astral plane.

- Magickal workings include enhancing symbolic dreams from the spirit world, starting an art project, bringing forward intuition, and elevating imagination.
- Sign: Pisces

CANDLE MAGICK OILS

- Basil: Energy
- Cinnamon: Sexual power
- Lavender: Self-love
- Rosemary: Healing
- Lemongrass: Bliss
- Peppermint: Success
- Sandalwood: Internal peace
- Vervain: Abundance

HOT TIPS

- Make sure to burn out your candle or wait until it extinguishes itself. Use the same safeguarding you would with any fire.

- Carve your name, initials, or a symbol that is associated with your intention into the candle. For example: if you are doing a spell to bring forward money, carve a dollar sign.

- Sometimes it's effective to repeat certain spells with the same candle. It can create a hypnotic rhythm and energy.

- Roll your candle in incense or herbs that you believe have magickal properties.

HOW A BLACK CANDLE CHANGED
MY LIFE FOREVER

As a teenager in the early 2010s, I obsessed over Harmony Korine's relationship with Marilyn Manson. Manson loved Korine's movie *Gummo*. Manson was the only artist alive that I felt I could connect with. I felt isolated from society, like a weirdo in my community, and persecuted for my strangeness—all traits for which Manson was being celebrated. He was a champion for everyone who felt ostracized. Reading about artists like Manson in magazines is how I felt less alone, because there were no artists around me.

When I was sixteen, I would compulsively replay an *MTV News* clip on YouTube of Manson talking about *Gummo* and how twisted Harmony is. I was jealous of Harmony because I wanted Manson to think that way about me. Harmony annoyed me because I didn't think of his work as groundbreaking. I thought of it as an aesthetic exercise—an ability I already had within me—and I didn't want his work to pollute my own burgeoning voice as an artist. None of the images in *Gummo* or *Kids* ever really did anything for me. I felt a lot of people were programmed to like him without knowing why. It felt like a hipster thing. The public celebration of his "genius" pissed me off, and I felt very competitive towards him. (Note: I saw *Spring Breakers* in the theater thirty times.)

A year later, I said aloud to myself: "Watch. The next young director Manson is going to co-sign publicly in the next five years is going to be me. I don't know how, but I am going to do this. Maybe it won't happen until I turn twenty-three, but it's going to happen."

When I was twenty and had just started to practice magick, a friend of mine told me she met Manson at a party and had gotten his number. "Give it to me right now," I said. "I need to work with him." I was consciously mimicking Manson himself, who as a journalist had strategically interviewed Trent Reznor as a way to advance his own music career. Maybe he would appreciate my assertiveness. This friend knew how much that opportunity meant to me, so she gave me his number, and I texted him.

Later that night, I lit a black candle and did a spell. I visualized the screen of my Blackberry lighting up as it received a response from Manson, and I imagined what that would feel like. It was the night of his birthday. I called on my guides, saying "I really need this right now. I need to collaborate with him."

I completed the spell and tried to forget about it, but I kept pacing around the house, super excited about what could happen. Eventually, after exhausting myself, I was like, "Fuck this. He's not responding. Maybe the spell didn't work. Witchcraft is bullshit."

I left my phone in the kitchen and crawled into bed. As I was falling asleep, my Blackberry text alert went off. I looked at my phone.

"Hey. It's MM. Sorry been with J. Depp. Crazy night."

I was euphoric. "This is it. I've shattered reality. I'm doing it. This is everything in all the books about witchcraft I've read. Magick is real. From this day on, I am doing candle magick forever."

I asked him for his email to send my idea and treatment for a real-time Snapchat movie. He got it and responded that night, saying: "I love it. Let's do this."

I was naïve at the time because I was unaware of the spiritual trials that can befall you. Entities create challenges to test your willpower and see if you can overcome them to get to where you want to go—to bring order to the chaos.

From the January night we began talking and discussing the idea until that summer, I worked on the project. It was trial by fire. Major models signed on and then dropped out. Just as soon as I seemed to be moving forward, things would come off the rails. I was feeling hopeless. Manson said to me during the process "You have spirit. You remind me of me. Remember, I didn't get where I wanted to be overnight. It's all going to work out. Trust me."

This was reassuring. I still had some divine hope.

After being straight up gaslit by a Hollywood producer who had set up fake meetings with me just to write down my ideas so he could pursue them without me, (which followed getting cursed out on the phone and called "some stupid kid who is never going to make it" by the business partner of one of the biggest horror movie directors of this generation), I decided to access my divine will and inner wrath and do the Snapchat movie on my own. I cast @internetgirl off of Instagram at two in the morning and sent her the script. I called her up, and she agreed to do it. Two of her witch friends helped out. I directed the film on FaceTime in my sister's apartment.

The end result, *Snapchat:Mudditchgirl91*, was a social experiment that centered around the concepts of "real" and "fake." It came from my belief that Instagram and social media are designed to exploit traumatized people. It was inspired by Amanda Bynes's public meltdown and because I recognized traits of Histrionic Personality Disorder in young people today and saw a lack of empathy in how people were responding to the situation.

Marilyn Manson ended up posting the premiere of the movie on his socials with the caption, "I have no idea why, but I know I like it."

My hyper-focus on Harmony and Manson's relationship ended up acting as a subconscious hyper-sigil in the world. After he watched *Snapchat:Mudditchgirl91*, he told me, "This is pure genius. This made me nervous." Someone who grew up being made nervous by Manson's music videos had made Marilyn Manson nervous. How does this happen? Candle magick!

My Snapchat movie was about a post-*Gummo* world and about kids who grew up wanting to stylize and direct their lives like they saw in Gaspar Noe, Sofia Coppola, and Harmony Korine films. If anything, I was mocking Korine's aesthetic and artists like him. I was eye-rolling at everything because I felt the democratization of "weird art" on the internet was so vapid and soulless.

Thanks to *Snapchat:Mudditchgirl91's* success, I was on the news section in *Vice*'s Snapchat story, *BroBible*, *i-D*, *Playboy*, *Oyster*, and *Paper* all in one week. The only other time I'd seen this type of thing happen was for major artists, so this was an absolute thrill. The film has even been featured in academic texts like Nancy Jo Sales's *New York Times* bestseller *American Girls*. None of that would have been possible without the power of Marilyn Manson and magick. (Note: Harmony, two years prior to this, had told me "Never stop making films…")

Later, Manson and I collaborated on a few projects, and there has always been total fucking chaos before the finish line—extreme spiritual tests and trials that have challenged my physical state, willpower, identity, self-worth, and psyche. Some highlights include a "banned album campaign" for Manson's record *Heaven Upside Down* that I did behind his record label's back (occult icon Kembra Pfahler said, "This is amazing and beautiful work you are doing. This is real and American." Bret Easton Ellis said "These are radical. This shocked me.") and a *King Kong Magazine* cover with Ellen Von Unwerth. When the cover was released on the night of his moon sign, Manson said to me, "I'm always going to remember what you did for me. I'm never going to forget this." This was a peaceful, full-circle, life-changing moment for me because I was able to help someone who had done so much for me.

These days, I have a history of blowing up Manson's phone with my problems like an abandoned child who has an emotionally unavailable father. His advice is always so helpful, cunning, and spot-on that I can't help but want more guidance. He does call me "son," so how can I help myself? I still get chills when I recall him telling me, "You want to make your dent on this world. I know you do."

What if I didn't believe in magick? What if I never lit that black candle back in January 2015? All it takes is a little candle magick to change your life forever.

8

SIGIL MAGICK

Have you ever wanted to put magick in your hands? Like, literally? If so, sigil magick is just the trick for you. A sigil is a magick symbol representing one's private desire and intention, charged through one's willed energy to alter reality as well as his or her state of consciousness.

When you create a sigil, you are physically manifesting your intention. It's not rubbing a candle that already exists. It's creating something that didn't exist until you willed it. Sigil magick is a way to ground us and reconnect us to the power of magick and its existence.

Generally, sigil magick can be used to meet certain people or summon certain qualities in a person. Sigils can be used for healing and influencing the collective consciousness to create change. You can make a sigil to bring something into your life, to ask for a gift from the universe, or to banish something to protect yourself. You can even put a sigil beneath your pillow to invoke prophetic dreams. You can make a sigil to be used for prayer, as an offering, or to give thanks to spirits.

A sigil creates a new language that only you can understand. If anyone else saw it, they wouldn't know what the intention would be, and in today's highly exposed, reveal-all world, having something so private that only you understand can produce an almost euphoric feeling. For this reason, sigil magick can be rejuvenating spiritually and mentally.

Sigil magick is like setting an intention and assigning meaning to a bunch of code, like "953XZzew-062295-erp039r4o0-epd." It looks like hacker code, but to the practitioner, it might mean, "I am strong enough to move past the situation I got myself into with Aidan."

There is a powerful feeling when you are turning a desire into a symbol that only you can understand, and something cathartic about turning something only you can feel in your body into something physical. You feel free when you dispel and release your intention.

Sigil magick can be a heavy reminder of how images and words shape reality and change how we engage with the world around us. You know that weird reaction you felt in your body the first time you saw Aphex Twin's logo? That's the power of sigil magick at work.

Sigils are controlling us at all times. They are all around us. The logos for YouTube, Instagram, Twitter, and Facebook are all sigils that have been charged to charm people to give up their energy and time for artificial illusory highs of being seen and getting likes.

What the CEOs and corporations who charged these sigils don't want you to know is that you are just as powerful, and you have your own choice and will. You can be a part of the reversal of this process by creating your own sigils and charging them with power, whether it is for global change or simply for improving your own life. You should start to become conscious of all the sigils you are absorbing and consuming all the time.

Olly Alexander, the frontman of the pop band Years & Years, who has dropped many hints that he is out of the broom closet, clearly made a sigil for his band's *Palo Santo* album. When I realized Olly had done this, there was a sense of frustration because I didn't know what it meant or what he had charged it with. I was so curious, charmed, and entranced. This is the power of sigil magick.

MY EARLY DAYS OF SIGIL MAGICK

When I first discovered sigil magick, I was both terrified by it and ecstatic over it. As a sexually active twenty-year-old, I didn't have many reservations about starting right away, since the most common way of charging a sigil is through the hit of an orgasm. But I was a bit conflicted. One part of me said, "Wow. I mean, of course shooting your load while you think of a symbol in your mind to get what you want is how you do magick. I'm sure Trent Reznor has done this a lot in his life." The other part of me said, "Well, Alex, this is where you are at in life—jerking off in your parent's basement to magickal symbols. Have you hit a new low? Is this what giving up on life is?" And yet, somehow, this all felt integral to my awakening as a witch because there is something so powerful about engaging with a technology that has been around for thousands of years and discovering it for the first time. Honestly I've always been a fucking weirdo, but I really outdid myself by jerking off to symbols and shooting my intention load out into the universe.

Sigil magick is something I only do when I feel intuitively drawn to it. Honestly, it's not something I ever felt truly comfortable doing because it always felt laborious and foreign. While other magickal practitioners are completely called to it, I was not. The last sigil I did was for an album campaign I art-directed for Baby Blue, a trans-female artist on the underground label Ascetic House. Baby Blue had experienced physical and psychological abuse at the hands of cis men, and we decided to work out these traumas through art. We made a sigil together and charged it with our intention of self-love and forgiveness. I put a lot of energy and love into this sigil. After we made the sigil, I got extremely sick. The last time I had gotten so sick was following another risky magickal occurrence. I quickly realized the error I had made. I didn't protect myself. If you want to televise your sigil to the masses, be wise and make sure you are protected, because this tool is powerful. When we practice magick, we are toying with the unknown, and we can never be 100 percent certain that there won't be repercussions.

Experimenting with sigil magick is a great reminder that magick is not about specifics. It has no laws, only intuitive aesthetics. You are the only one who gets to decide what tools work for you. Everyone has their own way of doing things, and there is nothing better than sigil magick to remind you of the beauty of free will.

When I think back on the memories of my first sigil magick rituals, it feels a bit like reflecting on a dream sequence version of me as a character in a witch movie where I am about to awaken my full potential and power. This process can be frightening, but it is also the exact type of path you end up on while invoking magick in your life. I associate sigil magick with a younger version of myself, feeling powerless and hopeless, masturbating to glyphs I learned from some pdf on Google. *Real nice, Kazemi.*

HOW TO DO SIGIL MAGICK

1. The only tools you will need are a pen and a piece of paper.
2. Write the words of a desire or intention onto the piece of paper. For example: "I am working on a magazine cover with Alice Glass."
3. Once the words are written out, remove all repeated letters and vowels. Using the example above, you'll be left with the following consonants: "KZVTH."
4. On the back, or on a different piece of paper, write out the letters and start to connect and re-arrange them into something that looks like an image creature beast, something mythological and witchy. As you create the symbol, cross out each letter you've incorporated. You don't need to worry about how it looks, just start to connect the letters together and morph them into a sigil.
5. Charge the sigil.
6. Activate the sigil.

Are you ready for some fun? Charging and activating the sigil is the point at which you transform it into a magickal tool. If you don't charge it, you're just going to have a bunch of lines on a piece of paper that have no meaning or power.

CHARGING A SIGIL

There are no limitations placed on the technology you choose to charge your sigil or to achieve a zero-mind state. A zero-mind state can be invoked with everything from sensory deprivation to hyperventilation and pain. Charging a sigil is a way to fill up your magickal symbol with energy.

You must power up your intent in order to manifest and create the change you want to see in your reality. I like to look at charging a sigil as launching it out into the universe.

At the moment you feel you've reached a zero-mind state, you need to see the image of your chosen sigil. This is the release, the launch, the projecting out and placing your trust into the unknown universe.

I have charged sigils by spinning to exhaustion to Aphex Twin and Squarepusher, via orgasm, and by accessing the inner angelic light beaming from my palms into the symbol.

Meditate intently on the sigil to activate its power, and feel that symbol being charged. Try imagining the color of your energy and that color emblazoning the sigil, whether it is blue fire or hot pink dust. Concentrate on the shape, hold that symbol in your mind, and banish other thoughts. Visualize both the outcome and the symbol, and as you are charging the image in your mind, burst it. It is important that you focus solely on the image in front of you. This will take practice and may not come easily, but, in time, you will be able to think of nothing else while you are charging your sigil with your desired end result.

In the case of Alice Glass, I was visualizing the feeling of opening a package containing the magazine, holding it in my hands, and people sending me pictures of it in stores.

You are trying to make sure your conscious mind will not remember doing this ritual, or what the sigil means, because you are putting your trust into the universe and the otherworld. Charging a sigil can be looked at as burying your intention so deep into your subconscious mind that it will listen to you and turn everything into action.

METHODS TO ACHIEVE A ZERO-MIND STATE

- Blast weird techno music like Aphex Twin, Squarepusher, or Boards of Canada while spinning yourself into a state of exhaustion. When you feel like you can't take it anymore, visualize the sigil being charged and infused with your desire.

- Watch a video of something you are really afraid of or something that will shock you. At the point of panic, visualize the sigil and release it.

- If you masturbate or have a partner in sex magick (more on sex magick coming soon—chill), visualize the symbol right before you orgasm to let it go. The moment of orgasm will clear your mind, and you'll literally feel your intention being charged and built up as you climax.

- Try to create an intense feeling inside of yourself. Access this feeling via pulling up a memory—whether it brought you pain, joy, or grief. Direct this energy into your sigil, and alchemize it into magickal energy. Listen to music that conjures strong feelings. Remember: You are willing yourself into a highly-charged emotional state.

ADDITIONAL WAYS TO CHARGE A SIGIL

- Try crystals. Rub the crystal over your sigil or absorb energy out of the crystal into your palm to press into your sigil.

- You can coat the paper of your sigil with oils to charge it. As you apply the oils, visualize the energy being infused into the paper.

- You can charge a sigil with a source of energy that comes from your body—either blood, semen, or saliva.

- Put your palm over the sigil, and visualize all of the energy in your body going into the paper.

ACTIVATING A SIGIL

After charging comes activation. An IMG model I know made a sigil to get a guy she liked to DM her back on Instagram. She charged it with orgasm, but it didn't work. She called me saying, "Why didn't you tell me that you have to burn the sigil? I didn't activate it!" She finally activated it, and twenty-four hours later the guy responded.

The purpose of sigil magick is to forget about it, and this purpose becomes physical once we activate the sigil. When we activate a sigil, we are sending it off into the magickal ether and trusting the sigil to work in our subconscious. This is the release of what has just been charged and symbolizes the destruction of the symbol. You want to forget that you ever did this. You want to forget your desire and intention, as if you were intruding on someone else's dream, seeing symbols and images that you won't remember once you depart. Every practitioner has their own way of destroying it.

A sigil is something that is meant to be buried and cremated in the depths of your subconscious. It is something that is so meaningless; so strange and confusing to your awakened rational mind. Some practitioners believe that sigils have the power to bypass your internal belief system. I believe that sigils interact with the astral plane without the hindrance of your "inner roommate" (that skeptical voice in your head that is cynical and jaded) influencing its power. It's like planting a mysterious, mystical seed into the universe that allows magick to grow within your own hands.

WAYS TO ACTIVATE A SIGIL

- Burn it.
- Flush it.
- Scatter its ashes into the wind.
- Put your sigil in a bowl of water with oils, and let it submerge and disintegrate.
- Bury your sigil into the earth.
- Now forget about it and move on. This never happened. Don't tell anyone about it or the sigil will lose its power. You don't even remember it, remember? *Thank u, next.*

SIGIL MAGICK INSTRUCTIONS

1. Identify your intention and desire.
2. Write it down.
3. Remove all the vowels and repeated letters to leave a string of consonants.
4. Write out the remaining letters and start to squish, connect, and rearrange them to the point where the only thing left is a magickal symbol/glyph.
5. Now begin to alter yourself to reach a zero-mind state by charging the sigil. Once the energy has boiled up to a point where you can't take it anymore, visualize the symbol in your mind—visualize your power and all your will being infused into that symbol.
6. Destroy the sigil. Rip it apart, flush it, burn it, or bury it.
7. Forget about the sigil. The magick has been activated. Snap out of it! Return to the world and out of the dreamlike state of consciousness you have willed into existence for your magick.

My sigil worked. I ended up working with Alice Glass. We did a cover together for *King Kong Magazine,* and I have a video on my computer of me freaking out while opening the boxes, in real life, on the other side of the spell I did. Alice's friend Shy styled the shoot, and she was incredible to work with. I think she was a witch, so to work with another magickal person on something I intended to manifest—and to help another witch out—was an honor.

HOT TIPS

- Assert yourself to the universe. Do not use "I will" or "I hope." Write "I am." I am is about the present tense. Believing the intention has already been manifested is the point of all magick.

- If doing traditional sigil magick is too overwhelming, try doing something simple like drawing a heart or a dollar sign. Draw any symbol connected to your desire and charge your intention with it, without making it into a gylph. Any symbol can become a sigil.

- Try different charging methods and learn what feels right for you. Remember: Charging = Infusing with Energy. Willing into Existence/Activating = Destroying and Forgetting!

- If your sigil doesn't look magickal facing up, turn the page around until you feel it looks more witchy—*Ancient Aliens* type shit. Try removing letters that are mirrors or inversions of other letters, such as M and W if both appear in the same statement on the paper. Try drawing a circle around your sigil or all your lucky numbers to the sigil!

9

ELEMENTAL MAGICK

Have you ever thought of what could happen in your life if you utilized the energies and powers of nature? Even many who don't practice or believe in magick are drawn to nature for its mystical healing properties.

Magickal practitioners try to become one with nature by communing with its power to unify our will with the magickal source of Earth to create change and produce results.

Elemental magick harnesses the energies within any of nature's four elements (detailed below) to assist you in accordance with your divine will.

- **Fire** represents the soul and will. It encompasses passion, destruction, transmutation, and enlightenment.
- **Earth** represents the material plane and all things physical. It encompasses prosperity, stability, and reinforcement.

- **Air** represents the intellect. It encompasses logic, knowledge, and communication.

- **Water** represents emotions. It encompasses love, friendship, adaptation, and reflection.

Elemental magick is one of the most fun systems because of how simple it is. Sometimes I leave a water bottle outside on a stormy night to collect rain. Then I use that rain in a full moon ritual, mixing it with oils for protection to connect me to the element of water. I had great experiences in my early days working with the element of earth, burying my intentions into the ground with seeds on new moons, and burning my intentions on pieces of paper with fire. I would light incense to connect me to the element of air while I meditated on abstract-outcome spells.

Some of the most empowering magick I have done was when touching ocean water and absorbing the natural energies into my palm, feeling the power going into my body. Whether it is on the summer solstice, sitting on a rock in front of the ocean and dipping my hands into the water to dress my candles, putting my palm up to a tree, or burning something into ashes, the elements function as batteries for all of my magick.

Elemental magick does not take much work. If you have a sink you can do a water ritual. If you have a lighter, you can do a fire ritual. If you have incense to burn, you can do an air ritual. If you have access to dirt, plants, flowers, and grass you can do an earth ritual. You get to decide what you correspond with each element. Do what feels best for you.

Remember: Even in elemental magick, what we use is still a prop. It's the power of your intention and will—the prop charged with *your* energy—combined with the forces of nature that make elemental magick so powerful.

HOW TO DO ELEMENTAL MAGICK

1. Find something that you associate with one of the four elements.
2. Set an intention that you believe corresponds with the element you want to use in a ritual. For example: Burn a piece of paper with the word "creativity" written on it for a fire ritual. Bury a seed with an item that represents your goal into the ground for an earth ritual. Light incense for an air ritual to bring upon new ideas. Put rainwater in a bowl for purification in a water ritual.

ELEMENTAL RITUAL LIST

The following are some of the traditional correspondences for the various elements, but you can establish your own set of attachments to each.

- **Fire rituals:** Magickal workings involving passion, creativity, and inspiration.
- **Earth rituals:** Magickal workings for success, prosperity, and fertility.
- **Air rituals:** Magickal workings for new ideas, knowledge, and charm.
- **Water rituals:** Magickal workings for purification, healing, protection, and relationships.

HOT TIPS

- Call on the elements before or while performing any ritual. Say each of them out loud. You might feel your body connect to the energies of the elements.

- Think of the element you have felt most associated with your whole life. Maybe you love going to the lake, building bonfires, or watching dandelions blow through the air. Build an attachment to the element you feel drawn to the most.

- Create magickal connections! If the full moon is in a water sign, try doing water rituals for powerful results. (Note: to learn what sign the moon is in, check one of the many moon calendar sites online.)

- Declare yourself open to nature and the power of magick. If you feel shielding the environment is a part of your path, continue to protect our Earth, and be one of our divine planet guardians who allows us to celebrate and experience all of the beautiful elements. Try putting your hands over a plant, and visualize the power of the plant going into your palms!

10

SEX MAGICK

What do you think of when you think of sex magick? Do you think of group sex in covens with goat heads and red candles? Do you think of powerful celebrities participating in forbidden Illuminati sexual acts in the dungeons of Beverly Hills? Do you think of horned-up teenage boys who listen to Ministry while reading spells off of the internet to try to get girls to sleep with them? I can confirm all of that stuff does indeed happen on planet Earth, but it has nothing to do with sex magick.

Sex magick is when we make the conscious decision to use our will to incorporate sex into a magick ritual. Yes, that means thinking of one of the most intimate acts as a means of manifesting what it is that you or your chosen sexual partner wants into the material plane. Just like making sigils, lighting candles, and working with the elements in the ways that work best for you, fucking can become a magickal act (especially on a Scorpio full moon!) too.

If you can orgasm, you can do sex magick. Sex magick is setting an intention or desire before sex and releasing what you would like to happen at the point of orgasm with yourself or with a chosen sexual partner. If you are going to orgasm anyway, you might as well alchemize that power to materialize what it is that you desire. The sexual energy within an orgasm is powerful and can be a potent ingredient in a magick ritual. Sex alters your state of consciousness and gets you to that magickally ripe zero-mind state. The moment of orgasm assists you with sending an intention, shooting it deep into the unknown as well as the depths of your mind. This is a time where most people feel time and space don't exist and are in total ecstasy.

Doing sex magick with someone can double the power of magick. It's double the energy, and double the energy means double the magick!

Sex magick can also be done alone and is commonly used during sigil magick, but you can bring yourself to orgasm without making a sigil and carry on with using the power of orgasm to manifest what you want in life.

You can do sex magick for anything that you want—to advance any area of your life that you choose or anything that corresponds with what your current true will or desire is. You do not need to utilize sex magick for more matches on dating apps, more sex, more love, or more sexual power. You can if that is your will, but sex magick can be used to do any type of magick.

The first time I do sex magick will be a spell for more success, productivity, or self-advancement. Yes, I am a twenty-five-year-old sex magick virgin. I have never practiced sex magick with someone else. I've never been able to do it because I think it's extremely risky, especially with someone you don't share an intimate bond with. You are subjecting yourself to someone else's energies and building a psychic link in a way that no other magickal act makes possible. I don't recommend practicing sex magick with people off of hook-up apps. I would share this act with someone you trust and feel a strong, intimate bond with, as that is said to create more powerful results from those I know who practice sex magick.

Sex magick is a great reminder that you are the only one who gets to decide what you consider to be an act of sex. Sex magick is not about traditional heteronormative and cis expressions of sexuality and desire. You, as a practitioner, get to choose what constitutes a sexual act. Oral and penetrative sex are not the only sexual acts that are valid. All sexual expressions and desires are valid if they are not harming anyone and are consensual. Do what makes you happy and horny.

Remember, too, that there is a lot of bullshit occult literature in which sex magick is about the union of the masculine and feminine (and the invocation of the goddess and god) which is very pagan, dogmatic, and traditional. If that is a valid sexual expression of sex magick for you, it is fine to honor those archetypes, but it does not need to be the template you follow, and you shouldn't let this old-school witchcraft shit fuck with your sex magick mojo.

MAGICKAL FLUIDS

The fluids produced by the human body can be used as magickal ingredients in sex magick with a chosen sexual partner. One's bodily fluids are the essence and physical materialization of their soul and can be a powerful and natural liquid to use in a spell. These can be anything from menstrual blood to cum and urine.

Using the fluids of someone else can be a way to symbolize and materialize something into their life. Some magickal practitioners ingest these fluids as a means of communion during sex magick, but you can also use magickal fluids to salve the body or to charge talismans and amulets so long as you charge the fluids with your magick and a specific intention.

I have buried my sperm in the ground to let the Earth do its natural work, to regenerate it, and to return it as something new and powerful. I have yet to drink someone's blood but wonder if Angelina Jolie and Billy Bob Thornton were regular practitioners of sex magick. Remember when Angelina broke headlines in the early 2000s wearing a vial of Thornton's blood around her neck?

Please be hyperaware of the health risks when playing with magickal fluids. Ask your doctor, "What are the risks if I swallow someone's blood?" You have to remember that ingesting bodily fluids has the same dangers as oral sex, so please make sure you are getting tested, and try to educate yourself on the risks and dangers. You don't want to transmit diseases out of curiosity or because of something you think will amp up your magickal practice. It won't be worth it.

HOW TO DO SEX MAGICK

1. Discuss your goal and intention with your chosen sexual partner. If you are alone, write it down on a piece of paper. If you are with your chosen sexual partner, discuss what it is that

you want to materialize during this ritual. Talk about what you want to do with the energy you are about to produce with each other. Have you decided if you are putting out intentions for the same or separate goals? For example, you could be doing a ritual to bring more money into your lives, or you could be doing a ritual for more joy, while your chosen sexual partner could be doing a ritual for more willpower.

2. Begin the sexual act. Focus on the energy being raised as you are altering your state of consciousness to reach a magickal zero-mind state.

3. When you are ready to orgasm, visualize your desired intention, then release your orgasm. You are aiming and directing that energy into this desire that will burst in your mind and body.

4. After you orgasm, let it be. When you feel the ritual is done, it's done.

HOT TIPS

- Respect your body and the bodies of others by getting tested and practicing safe sex. I know it's cool in our current culture to "raw-dog" and not use condoms, but I don't think it's worth putting your body in harm's way for something that is only going to be a temporary experience.

- If you aren't comfortable using orgasms with magick, try to visualize your intention or desire when doing something that makes you feel good and sexy, and not for anyone else but for you! Whether it's putting on a dress you look good in, feeling fresh in a new Hugo Boss shirt, doing your makeup, or looking at your muscles in the mirror after the gym, in this charged up state, do sex magick!

- You can use sex magick to invoke a pop archetype, modern entity, god or goddess that you feel connected with—whether it is Chris Hemsworth, Ezra Miller, Hayley Kiyoko, or Ariana Grande. You can visualize yourself as them or how you imagine they'd act in the bedroom to try to spice up your own sex magick. If you don't feel comfortable doing sex magick with someone else, try to imagine a sexual experience with a god, entity, or goddess you want to be with. Thank the energy, and maybe they'll come back for seconds!

- Beware of any partner who practices magick and says you have to do a particular sexual act in order for the spell to work. Sex magick is not about influencing someone's will. It's about consent and freedom—participating with someone else's will to create a powerful change in both of your realities. Respect boundaries and make sure everyone involved is safe and relaxed. It's not about feeling uncomfortable or pressured to do something you don't want to do in order to make your partner feel good.

11

HOW THE FUCK DO I KNOW WHEN MAGICK WORKS?

Magick appears in the natural world as a series of coincidences that correspond with the intention you cast out during a ritual. Magick often manifests itself in ways that you don't expect and likely don't recognize as connected to the spell you've cast. When you cast a spell, you can't just sit on your ass and wait. A real world application must be enacted that is related to your spell.

If I perform an abstract outcome spell for more career opportunities, I may *coincidentally* receive an email from someone looking to collaborate with me or my company. You have to remember that when your spells are manifesting and you start to receive the things you want, that is your spell working, and you caused this influence.

We do not know how or why magick works, but I will share some of my theories as to why it is effective.

1. I believe that when we do rituals we open ourselves up to the spirit world (angels, entities, demons) to whom we cast out our spells. They mold this energy into the material plane. These entities will then test our mental and physical endurance to see if we can prepare and change ourselves to go where we need to be in order to achieve our intended goal.

2. Our thoughts have vibration and power, and we can affect reality by choosing what thoughts to focus on and where to direct our energy. When we do magick, we are casting our power into the astral plane where it is reshaped before being returned to us in the material plane.

3. Magick is our birthright, and we can all influence and bend the natural order of events. Reality is malleable. Reality can be hacked by various spiritual systems, the most powerful of which is magick.

4. Every event in the universe was set before us. We are simply fulfilling our souls' paths. The magick and rituals that work are a part of those paths. You can study and see the astrological data, repeating coincidences, and patterns of destiny aligning in your life by looking at the daily transits.

5. Magick is self-hypnosis. We program our subconscious to accomplish the goal that we set out to achieve, and then we end up focusing on all the variables around us—the practical steps to get to the goal we intend to reach. Our conscious self becomes more aware of what needs to get done, and we end up accessing parts of ourselves that we might not have

been able to had we not entered this mesmerized state through magickal ritual.

Some magickal practitioners don't care about understanding how it works. They just pursue results guided by a hardcore conviction that it does work, in the same way Christians feel joy when their idea of God materializes the miracle that they wanted.

Magick is all about setting a ritual into action—creating the spark. If you do a self-love spell on yourself to attract more friends or romantic partners, you need to kickstart things by going to events, talking to people, and being social. There's a much higher chance you'll meet the kind of person you intended to. You can't just be like, "Bro, just did my spell. Someone hot is going to knock on my door." Unfortunately, life is not an early 2000s teen movie. You are just as much a part of your spell working as all your homies in the spirit world are.

There is nothing more euphoric in this world than when you are on the other side of reality, living inside of what you intended or visualized and feeling what you set out to feel. All the energy, all the proper moon phase planning and trust in the power of magick pays off. I have been inside of the results of spells, whether it's been hugging Taylor Swift, holding a magazine cover I created of Diplo in drag, getting this book deal, healing from the bindings of trauma, or a cab showing up when I needed it. I've lived inside of the rituals and feelings I intended to create, and that is how I know magick is real and reality is bendable.

Sometimes I like to test myself to see the mysterious places Magick can take me. On a Capricorn full moon, I did an abstract outcome spell for success in my journalism career. I didn't know what would happen, but, in my gut, I felt the spell was working. I put out the energy of believing that what I had done was going to take my career to the next level. A few weeks later, I wrote a piece about Selena Gomez's "Bad Liar" for *V Magazine*, praising the art she and Petra Collins were creating together. I felt represented and understood by the work, and I had to do something celebratory and productive with that feeling. A few weeks after that, on an Aries waxing moon—which I later learned was Selena's moon sign—I got an email from Selena's publicist asking me to interview her and Petra Collins together for a feature in *Dazed Magazine*. If I had never written the piece about her in *V*, I would never have been noticed, but it was all connected to the spell I had cast in the first place. I have always felt a tremendous connection to Selena since we are both Cancers, and, to my magickal shock, Selena and I got to talk about what it's like to be a Cancer and how it can be frustrating feeling so much, that we end up creating perceived feelings and have to sort through our emotions to figure out what is real and what is not. That was a magickal moment.

SIGNS TO LOOK OUT FOR WHEN YOUR MAGICK IS MANIFESTING ITSELF

1. When a spell is starting to manifest, it can feel like total chaos. You might do something out of the ordinary that will take you out of your daily routine but will then lead you to an event that is bringing you closer to your intended result. Opportunities will come forward in ways that disrupt your life. I believe this is because time is nonlinear. It's more of a color, a construct. It's an idea rather than a fixed thing.

2. You might be driven by an intuition to go somewhere you wouldn't normally go or do something you hadn't been planning to do that results in something surprising. This has happened to me countless times with parties I hadn't wanted to go to but then forced myself to and ended up meeting someone who turns out to be a big part of my life going forward.

3. It may feel like a *coincidence*, but it's not. It's a result. You deserve to feel the excitement of that magickal synchronicity, and you deserve to stitch that event together with your ritual and see how all the data fits together. When you start practicing magick, stop thinking of coincidence as coincidence. Think of it as a result.

The first couple of times I felt magick worked for me, I thought it was beginner's luck. But then I kept doing it, and it kept working. I knew then that I would be a complete fool to ignore these powerful results. The best part about it was that it was coming from *me*. I was creating the reality that I wanted to live in through these rituals, and I was getting the things that I wanted. The combination of a practical, hard-work ethic and the power of magick has enabled me to achieve goals on a regular basis. The chaos that might manifest from a ritual may not be what you intended, but it may be what you needed to learn something or to evolve on your spiritual journey as a soul in this lifetime.

I felt alone at first because I wanted everyone around me to be using this divinity I had tapped into. Not everyone is open to receiving or practicing magick. It's something that I've had to accept. And older witches aren't always receptive to giving advice or discussing theories on why magick works. Don't diminish the power of what you've experienced if you feel dismissed by others. Share your powerful results with magickal friends you trust who have opened up about their practice and results with you, or just keep it between you and the entities. I'm sure they'd like it that way, anyway!

EXAMPLES OF HOW MAGICK MANIFESTS

1. Female-identifying practitioner does a specific outcome spell to attract a romantic partner on the Libra new moon. This practitioner sets out the intentions of the qualities she wants in a girlfriend. Practitioner downloads Tinder and, coincidentally, gets super-liked by almost the exact dream girl she visualized and is now feeling a resurgence of the energy she imagined when she envisioned the spell working.

2. Male-identifying practitioner does an abstract outcome spell for more willpower on the Leo full moon. The practitioner coincidentally feels the urge to go to the gym and start working on his body, which is the ultimate test of his willpower. He is now making gains in the gym and feeling a resurgence of the energy he imagined when he envisioned the spell working.

3. Non-binary identifying practitioner does a specific outcome magick spell to attract a job opportunity. The non-binary practitioner goes out with their sibling for dinner and coincidentally learns of an opening at a friend's company. They are now feeling a resurgence of the energy they imagined when they envisioned the spell working.

HOW A SPELL MANIFESTED FOR ME

I did a spell on the Scorpio full moon. The spell was to meet someone with the astrological placement "Mars in Scorpio." My intention and the energy I sent out was the feeling of my spell working, "The spell worked! I met someone with Mars in Scorpio!"

Two weeks later, I spoke to a girl in a department store about astrology. I did not know her, but she told me she is a Pisces.

A friend invited me to a party on a Scorpio waxing moon. At the party, I think I see the girl from the department store. It wasn't her, but we started talking. After a while, I asked about her astrological chart. Turned out she has Mars in Scorpio! Reality glitched. The spell worked.

WHY DID MY MAGICK NOT WORK? WHAT'S WRONG WITH ME?

You are not any less powerful because a ritual didn't work. When you don't receive something you set out to materialize, the ritual will almost always teach you something about yourself that prepares you to change or to receive something better that ends up being what you needed. The journeys my rituals have sent me on have brought me to people I never thought I'd meet, places I'd never thought I'd go, and challenges I never believed I would face. A magickal ritual always creates chaotic nexus points that challenge you and bring you further into alignment with your soul's purpose. Sometimes we aren't ready to receive the result we intend to materialize. It may be that we have to grow and evolve to catch up with it.

This is why I follow the belief, via my own discovery, that magick *always* works, even if I don't get what I intended. I learn something about myself, and that knowledge brings me to a place beyond where I set out to go. I am protecting myself through my own divinity.

I am not telling you to believe anything. Your beliefs belong to you and are created by you through your interpretation of your own experiences. Nothing is fixed in the world of theory. There have been so many times where I've done rituals for certain outcomes, and when I didn't receive that outcome, I realized I didn't actually want that outcome and was grateful to not have received it. I believe we get everything we need when we need it from magick.

Fear and doubt are the last things you should ever bring into a ritual. There is a lot of perfectionism-anxiety in the occult community today. Some people believe that the reason spells didn't work the way they wanted them to is because the practitioner wasn't clear enough in how he or she visualized the desired result, or maybe somehow, someway the individual could have prevented that chaotic coincidence that was connected to the results. I don't believe this one bit. I think the universe and spirit world are full of chaos. When you send your energies out to the celestial and astral worlds, anything can happen. You must be responsible for the risks you take through your ritual work.

Magick works when you let go. As soon as I have given up or have forgotten about the ritual, suddenly what I wanted or needed appears in my reality. I have no idea why this is. If you are too attached and keep thinking about it, it messes up your magick. If you just let go and be super chill, you are more likely to get a successful result.

OMFG! MY SPELLS KEEP WORKING.
AM I POWERFUL NOW?

Your rituals keep working. The magickal results are pouring in, and you are basically an angelic entity living your dream life. Are you powerful now? I can't answer that. Only you can. I struggle with this concept. It seems a little histrionic to walk around with an inflated ego because you believe you have magickal powers, but if that's what works for you, go for it. I have been referred to as powerful by witches, tarot readers, and magickal alchemists, but I believe everyone has magickal power within them. I'm not sure if any of us can gauge the level of another's power. There's an unlimited resource of entities and elements.

Magick is about seeing the higher meaning, the invisible purpose in what happens when you stitch together the sequence of events that happen in your life. You see, you are always on a road to somewhere greater, even in total suffering. You are on a path to a higher place. Your past becomes an order. You can rearrange the order of events and bring order to chaos.

WHAT ABOUT ALL THE VARIABLES?

Maybe the spell worked because of the entity you called on, the moon phase, the emotions you put towards it, or the fact that you decided to fast and drink only honey and water before that particular ritual. What makes practicing magick so mysterious is that no one fucking knows why or how this works.

12

MAGICKAL ALCHEMY

Magickal alchemy is using your divine will to regenerate feelings and emotional states. It's the conscious choice to view your feelings and emotions as alchemical magickal states that can be used as potent ingredients in rituals. It's turning negative into positive and putting your weaknesses through the same process that turns lead into gold.

Magickal alchemy begins with viewing your emotions as base material that can be transformed into your will. Your emotions and feelings can become something divine. Using your will, your emotions and feelings can be broken down, separated, and treated as energy that can return to you in a higher angelic form.

When we do magickal alchemy, we become the manufacturers of our emotional states, crystallizing distinct energies into material form. We stop being controlled by our emotions and feelings. We assert control over them and understand all emotions and feelings are power and energy coursing through our bodies. All emotions and feelings are potent magickal power and ammo that can be redirected, recreated, and transmuted.

A state of self-destruction, such as a desire to sit in your room self-hating, can be turned into something constructive like going for a run or working on a task that needs to get done. You can wed your feelings and emotions to create powerful personal desires, purposes, and constructive aims. When we become conscious of our emotions and feelings, isolate them, and view them as magick ammo, we can reassess them and say, "What magick can I use this for?"

Alchemy is the most important part of my magickal process. I use alchemy almost every hour of the day. I am open to feeling everything—even if it's destructive or harmful—because I use my will to change those feelings and turn them into something more powerful or to illuminate something about me that can help myself or others. Emotions are unused magickal power that can be accessed.

This is why I live a straight-edge lifestyle. I couldn't bear to numb any feeling or emotion. It'd be like allowing a demonic hand to take the magick out of me. Whether it's self-loathing, euphoria, disappointment, or joy, I want all of it because they are tools to focus into an artistic project or ritual. I feel the energy coming back to me as something powerful.

There have been times when I felt a surge of creative inspiration, and I wasted it, soaking it on the dance floor instead of staying at home working. When it was over, I wished I had used those feelings to steal away in art rather than staying up all night with people I didn't like.

If you use magickal alchemy in your daily life, your life will change. View your emotions as potent liquids in your magickal cabinet. You have to capture these states, freeze them, and lock them away in the digital cabinet in your body. They are now tinctures and elixirs, stored in vials.

EXAMPLE OF DAILY MAGICKAL ALCHEMY

I am on the train thinking of someone who has wronged me. I am feeling my whole body ready to burst into flames. I grab my magickal necklace. I close my eyes and visualize this energy as the color red. Now I think of this color red transforming into silver. This silver intention and will is to bring me more willpower to help me finish my book.

HOW TO DO MAGICKAL ALCHEMY

1. Isolate your emotions and feelings.
2. Pulverize them and convert them into energy. Strip them of their usual connotations.
3. Assign a color to the energy and send it out of yourself.
4. Imagine this color returning to you as a different color along with something that you desire and want.

It can be helpful to create an equation of how you are going to convert the color of the energy, in combination with your will, into a new color. Visualize this process of energy changing and being sent back to you and filling your body up. See it change in your mind, and assign a result to it.

See the equation example below.

Red (revengeful feelings right now) + My will to change
the color = Silver (productivity)

LIST OF ALCHEMICAL STATES TO CONVERT

Manipulation	→	Willpower
Revenge	→	Self-Love
Rejection	→	Self-Approval
Sadness	→	Gratitude

ALCHEMICAL JEWELRY

Every time I am in an emotional state in which I feel destructive,
I hold onto a magickal necklace, press my finger down on it, and
start to do alchemy. When you have a magickal piece of jewelry to
remind you of your inner power to alchemize, you can use it easily
anytime. You can press down on this piece of jewelry whenever
you feel an intense alchemical emotion coming on or when you
are in the thick of it. With enough practice, you can use this cue to
perform magickal alchemy, on the go, wherever you are.

HOW TO CREATE ALCHEMICAL JEWELRY

1. Find a ring or necklace that you consider to be magickal or
   divine.
2. Bless the necklace or ring in salt water or hold it up to moonlight. Say aloud: "I am using this magickal tool to advance my

life through alchemy. I will remember my ability to alchemize
when I see this tool."

3. Visualize your energy and power going into it.
4. Start to alchemize in your daily life by pressing down on the
talisman and doing alchemical magick.

FROM BOY TO ALCHEMIST

I remember the first time I heard "Sleep to Dream" by Fiona
Apple. There was a rage that filled my body to the point I felt like
I could stab someone. This was a powerful misdirected alchemical
moment in my life, but by some odd intuition I felt I needed to seal
that emotion in my inner-digital magickal alchemy cabinet. I can
still access it from a vial with a label that says "FA2012.alchemy."
I've used it for successful magick, and since that experience, I've
stored and sealed away many emotions and feelings that I perceived as future magickal power. Before doing magickal alchemy,
I would stab my carpet and feel my rage going into the knife,
thinking of the people who I perceived as perpetrators of abuse.
I follow a controversial spiritual belief that I am not a victim of
anything, and that even though traumatic events are out of my
control, I created these trials and chose this soul before I came to
this Earth, to fulfill, survive, and level-up.

I feel everything. I want pain, joy, resentment, fear, anger,
sadness. I want to survive every state of being I am in. To numb
or void any emotion or feeling is to destroy endless possibilities for
alchemy and magick.

Before using magickal alchemy, I was incapable of seeing beyond my intense emotions. I could not recognize that my actions had unintended and destructive consequences.

This is what the song "Not Enough Violence" that I wrote with Ariel Pink was about. When I said *"halfway spinning to a better place in the body of a man/mind of a girl,"* I was talking about feeling persecuted by society for my ability to feel things so extremely. I was made to feel ashamed for my receptivity. My sensitivities were viewed as weak and embarrassing. I was nineteen, and I felt the fevers my own feelings were giving me were isolating. I wanted someone to "come into my world, and come into my experience." Ariel understood that about me and gave me a voice.

I now know I'm complex and can't be defined, but there was freedom when I realized all this intense emotion was just magickal energy blocked up inside of me that needed a healthy, nourishing outlet. I always felt like I recognized myself in highly emotional artists like Banks, Fiona Apple, Shirley Manson, Trent Reznor, Marilyn Manson, and Kurt Cobain. These artists are all alchemists. Creating art is one of the most effective forms of alchemy.

ARIANA GRANDE IS A POWERFUL MAGICKAL ALCHEMIST

Magickal alchemy is a way to bring order to chaos. Ariana Grande is a great example of someone who has done that.

In 2018, she had a plan that she shared with the world. Grande believed she was going to marry Pete Davidson. She believed she had found her soulmate, but the universe had a different plan. One of the loves of her life, Mac Miller, unexpectedly overdosed, bringing flames to her engagement.

How did she bring order to the chaos? Alchemy.

Ariana Grande went into the studio and alchemized her grief and trauma into her most successful album yet, *thank u, next*. She reclaimed her narrative. This was all done while grappling with alchemical liquids: the pressures of stardom, the trauma of the Manchester Arena bombing, Mac Miller dying, her engagement getting called off, and everyone expecting an explanation from her, all while being dehumanized in the press.

What we can learn from Ariana Grande is that when our plans devolve into chaos, we have the choice to survive and be divine.

Anytime in your life in which you have survived painful trials or a chaotic life disruption and chose not to be defined as a victim, you changed reality and became a stronger version of yourself. You remixed the situation you'd been given and became the best version of you by choosing how to respond to the painful event. You did magickal alchemy. You did magick to bring order to chaos. To quote Ariana—the alchemist princess herself: *"Come through like the sweetener you are, to bring the bitter taste to a halt."*

HOT TIPS

- When in a state in which you feel you need to dispel energy, whether it's to react in a destructive way to someone or when you are overjoyed, remember the affirmation RAT: redirect, alchemize, and transmute. Repeat "RAT" to pause yourself. Then reassess your reaction. The option to create magick is within you the second you feel what you feel.

- Call on your spirit guides/angels to ask for help in your alchemical process. If you don't feel strong enough to alchemize something, ask them to take this state or feeling away from you and bring it back to you as something new.

- You can create the sweetener Ariana is talking about on her album with the movement of your body and hands. Rub your hands together to produce heat, and, as you do, visualize yourself being sprinkled with angelic light; or use this special Pop Magick technique during an alchemical process.

- If you have created something while channeling your emotions, you've done alchemy. This could have been a chaotic event or a painting, but you did magick. You created something that wasn't there before. You get to choose whether you want to use your reactiveness for the force of good.

13

LOVE MAGICK ALCHEMY

Do you remember the first time you fell in love? I mean *really* fell in love. Maybe you stared down at your phone screen and felt a sense of panic when you saw their pic. They linked to their Instagram, so you spent all night stalking every piece of social media history that exists about them. Maybe you even asked for their birth time to check your astrological compatibility to understand why you have never experienced such an intense spiritual soulmate bond with someone. You feel your astral bodies becoming one when you look into their digital eyes. You see all the past lives you've spent together, and there is no way you are going to let them get away. All the moments you knew you found the one, all the angels sending you signs through repeating numbers, long, all-night conversations, that feeling of finally understanding what all those songs on the radio are about… It's not so distant anymore.

It's happening for you, even if they aren't on the same continent as you. Maybe last night you weren't supposed to go to that party you saw on Facebook and then you ended up there, and there was that person that you have been waiting for your whole life. Or at least it felt that way. Oh, the joys of love in the late 2010s.

Love is magick. Love is a mysterious and powerful force that encompasses all things. It can be the feeling of hearing your favorite band and scream-shouting their songs, looking into your new puppy's eyes, hugging your best friend after sharing a secret, or going into nature and looking at your reflection in the river. Love, like magick, is everywhere when we open ourselves to it.

When you think of anything that you associate with love, your body can create a powerful emotional response. That means producing alchemical states and opportunities to create magick via redirection. The thought of what you associate with love can be used in ritual. The internal events you react to can change your reality.

Remember the first time you realized that there was someone out there with whom you could experience romance? How euphoric and powerful it felt to fulfill all of your wildest romantic fantasies?

What if you could capture and convert this power rather than releasing it? What if you thought of love energy that you hold the will to convert? What if you had the software inside of you to convert that Try_To_Date_Emotionally_Unavailable_Human. mp3 into Self_Love.wav? What if, when in the state of limerence, you could convert your spiritual urge to release and go from: Keep_Getting_Rejected.mp3 to Doing_Something_That_ Makes_You_Happy.wav.

Well, now you can, and all it takes is practicing some good ol' love magick alchemy.

Love magick alchemy is a process that one can employ when they become aware of the power of their love energy. When one locates the power of their love energy, they can use their free will and power to choose how and where this energy gets directed without romantic release (which is what modern society has pro- grammed us and taught us the purpose of feeling love is.) This is a decision a magickal practitioner makes themselves without the influence or conditioning of society.

Love magick alchemy is how I destroyed my automatic trau- ma-chip programming of approval addiction, breaking the exhausting toxic cycle of zero-to-one-hundred relationships, blaming others, and creating fantasy bonds with people. Love magick alchemy is how I got myself, my light, and my life returned to me after giving and wasting magickal energy away in the wrong places. Once I isolated my desire to feel love and be loved and directed it towards myself, my reality changed in ways I couldn't believe were possible.

I used to be the type of person who would go to a party only for the opportunity to meet my soulmate. I lived in a fantasy world.

Love magick alchemy is not for everyone. Love magick alchemy requires discipline, delayed gratification, and accountability.

IT WASN'T ALWAYS SELF-LOVE FOR ME

When I was seventeen, Lana Del Rey told me that I reminded her of the kid from the movie *Almost Famous*. "You're fucking crazy. You know everyone. It's amazing." This was when I was the Music

Editor of *SuperSuper! Magazine,* a UK pop culture and fashion magazine that was a cult hit in London's trendiest scenes.

Lana and I used to email each other when I was in high school. She would check in to see how I was doing and encouraged me to watch *American Beauty*. I talked about everything with her: art, her music, my aspirations as an artist, films, and astrology. I told her that her music inspired me to sneak out and be bad in the suburbs but also how sad it made me that there was a self-awareness to my choices—that I felt as if I was art directing my teen experience. That felt depressing and impure because of the conscious focus on aesthetics of all the people around me.

I remember talking to her on my Blackberry in class, checking to see if she was going to respond and feeling anxious if she wasn't replying. "Did I do something wrong? Does Lana hate me now?" I felt like I had to push to receive reassurance from her so that I would feel good, or safe, again.

I felt special when I spoke to Lana even though I realized she was talking to a lot of people all the time. I felt addicted to the validation I received from her because I felt like I was whole when we talked. I look back now feeling sad for my seventeen-year-old self. I deserved to see myself and feel valid without an external source making me feel real or good enough.

I wasn't yet aware of why I was so desperate for approval. Since that time in my life, the trials I have created for myself have always stemmed from a pursuit to fill the loneliness I was feeling. I've searched for this feeling of love, of being connected and understood, to the point where I risked my reputation, happiness, health, bank account, and more to sustain, maintain, and fertilize the feelings of deep-connection I saw around me. It only ever came in glimpses—short euphoric bursts that would take me to the depths of nothing. I felt my life was controlled by the highs and lows of when someone approved of me rather than there being any stability, and the inconsistency of everyone else around me was a way for me to not be accountable for my role in my life.

Growing up working in the fashion/music industry since I was fifteen, I learned quickly that Hollywood is built upon approval addiction. You are chasing the next high of someone helping to elevate your career. "Here's Drake's number. Tell him I gave it to you. Maybe you could send him some ideas!" It's like buying a ton of lottery tickets and scratching, endlessly hoping for the big score, but always coming up empty.

In my early twenties, I became a magnet to excruciating, highly charged, intimacy-vacant toxic friendships and relationships.

I would to go to a party, find an object of desire—sexual, romantic, or platonic—and begin losing myself to them, as if they were a rare mythological creature. I wouldn't know why, but I would be so excited and so passionate. *I finally found someone I connect with. We are going to be best friends. We are going to talk about music and art together.*

I was carrying around this hungry ghost who believed love was the solution. The ghost would whisper that I would be healed through love. Love was the ultimate force that would keep me distracted and free me of all the pain that I was afraid to confront.

I'd end up draining all of my magickal energy, all summer long, into emotionally unavailable people, putting pressure on them to love me, and they would just become more distant. It got to a point where people were kicking me out of their houses, but I would still be there, begging for love, validation, and acceptance.

I lived in a constant state of disappointment, sitting around thinking, *You were supposed to show up for me, but you didn't.* I'd go into a panic after checking their Instagram story only to discover they were doing something that completely contradicted what they'd been showing to me. I'd feel so confused and angry at myself. *Why the fuck are you even thinking of this when there is so much work to get done?*

I was on a hunt to find myself in everyone I met. I tried so hard to fall in love with parts of me through discovering them in others, but it never worked. I could never regulate.

I was just so obsessive, so unaware, so unknowing that I was distracting myself, and I didn't even get to know anyone I let into my life because I was focusing on my idealized view of them. I was so narcissistic, selfish, and backwards. I would see qualities in people that weren't actually there as a way to justify my ability to fantasize about them more, therefore distracting myself more from the reality of the unaddressed, unresolved trauma chip inside of me that was running the show.

Looking back now with the knowledge I acquired in rehab, this makes sense to me. It's pretty simple. When you are traumatized and sick, the more intense the experience and the more a roller-coaster ride your emotions become.

I used to spend my days listening only to love songs, hoping that I would be made into a full person when someone would be there for me, whether it was a best friend or romantic partner. Now I listen to romantic music aware that I am worth obsessing over, being in love with, and taking care of. I deserve as much time as I want to heal and recover, and to be reborn.

The words of approval I wanted to hear from outside of myself were inside of me. Now, that's love magick alchemy.

LOVE MAGICK ALCHEMY EXAMPLE

Everyday

You see someone you think you could date on Tinder/Instagram. You feel limerence and are filled with romantic desire; you've noticed it.

Options

A. "I have captured this feeling and will change it from red to gold. I am going to do a self-love bath."
B. "I am going to try to go on a date with this person."

Choose option A: "I am going to do a self-love bath for myself tonight and read a book."

Ritual Magick

You are alone and romantic feelings are being activated. You feel limerence and are filled with romantic desire.

Options

A. "I have captured this feeling. I am changing it from red to gold. I am going to do a sigil magick ritual."
B. "I'm going to stalk an ex on Instagram for hours."

Choose option A: "Make a sigil and do a magick ritual directing towards a goal."

HOW TO DO LOVE MAGICK ALCHEMY

1. Get into a state of love, or think of a time when you had an idealistic crush on someone—an appetite for romance that needed to be satiated. Only you know the things that get you charged up with love, so access and think of those things.
2. Think of this state, energy, and feeling as something you are going to capture. You can either think of it as going fishing and using a worm to catch a fish, or think of it like something out of Pokémon, where you capture Pokémon in the wild and secure that Pokémon in the Pokéball. You are locking down that feeling.
3. Visualize the feeling being locked down. Assign a color to that feeling and imagine it changing into a different color that has now alchemized into a potent new energy. This is going to give you the power to redirect your romantic/love desire and emotion elsewhere. Visualize that power filling up your body to motivate you and drive you. This can be directed towards anything from a career goal to a sigil magick ritual.

LOVE MAGICK ALCHEMY RITUALS

Go on a magical date with yourself: Take yourself on a magickal date into the woods or a spot in nature. Anywhere you feel is magickal! It could even be somewhere in your house. If you haven't had the best luck with romance or have had traumatizing situations of unrequited love, realize that this time is set for you. Bring your favorite food, watch your favorite movie, or dance to your favorite songs. Ask yourself questions about yourself, and really get to know you and take time for you because you've earned and deserve this time.

Reawaken your passion: Romance and relationships are looked at as the ultimate goals in our world, but sometimes we forget that we can use all of that romantic passion and alchemize it into something beyond ourselves. Try to reconnect and reawaken any passions you have that have always felt like they brought you purpose, and look within yourself to find something that makes you feel independent and secure. When we are constantly being rejected by people on dating apps, it can feel like we are not worth anything, but that couldn't be further from the truth. Your passion will remind you of what you have in you, which is a will to create and be divine.

Charm yourself with self-love: A self-love ritual is a powerful magick gift to give to yourself in a world and society that is designed to make you feel self-loathing. You may have had experiences in which you feel damaged or wounded. Try to do a self-love spell in which you visualize a version of yourself who is confident and full of self-respect and love and is forgiving for the past mistakes and empty situations you might've gotten yourself into.

LOVE MAGICK ALCHEMY EXERCISE

1. Bring yourself to a state of limerence by thinking of a past love experience, a powerful romantic experience, or a discovery that aroused you.
2. Feel that energy, and hold it without letting it take you over. Think of it as something that just is, and let it exist. You don't need to assign good or bad or hot or cold.

3. Now, in that state of charged up romantic desire, focus on a self-care activity or love, or anything that is a pursuit of goals, or something that is nourishing that makes you happy—anything that is not a traditional romantic release.

A LIST OF TASKS TO DIRECT LOVE ENERGY TOWARDS

- Yourself
- Ritual
- Creating something
- Your friends
- Exploring nature
- Exploring your interests

HOT TIPS

- Are dating apps burning you out? Maybe it's time for a detox. You don't have to meet someone on a dating app. Be more social. Put yourself out there in real life more, and see who is interested. Maybe it's easier to talk to someone hot when you already know they've swiped right on you, but we all know that doesn't guarantee anything real or long term.

- A lot of people I know use Instagram and Tinder to build idealistic bonds with people in different cities, in which they are worrying and thinking about the life of someone on a different continent rather than in their own neighborhoods. If you use social media to astral-travel and create cyber-flames as a means to distract or avoid the reality and fear of dating people in your city, you are only hurting yourself. If you are meant to meet these people you've been talking to from all around the world, you will, but until then, try to challenge these new-world urges. Love magick alchemy is about not wasting what you are being pulled towards and becoming more conscious of your powerful emotional states of being.

- If you spend time stalking your ex or someone who didn't choose you back, you are hurting your magick, self-worth, and self-esteem. You are so much better than typing in the handle of that person who didn't choose you. You are so much better than trying to check up on who is in their life now. Why would you even need to know about that? Try to induce self-hypnosis, and pretend it's 1985—a time where these means of stalking are not available.

- Do you believe in soulmates? I do, but I believe we have to do work on ourselves in order to receive, access, or reach them. Magick is all about transforming yourself to transform reality. If you haven't had the best luck in romance, try to get some help from a therapist or dedicate an area of your life to evolution, and work on becoming the best version of you.

14

SEX MAGICK ALCHEMY

Do you remember the last time you were horny? I mean *really* horny, to the point where you felt like you needed to masturbate or have sex to be freed of the feeling. Full of desire and lust, running on autopilot, you could feel the shift from where you were before to when you got horny and, god fucking damn, it is as if you suddenly became a different person. Maybe it was someone hot on the street that made you bite your knuckle, or you were just scrolling on your phone in bed on YouTube or Instagram and boom!— there you are opening tabs on PornHub, feeding into this horny feeling, and then releasing it. Or maybe you are re-downloading Tinder or Grindr after deleting it 150 times, looking for anyone to come over to fuck or just going in for a quick sext session during your break at work so you can be freed of this horniness.

What if you had the discipline, focus, and will to choose how you use this invisible energy we identify as being horny? What if you switched the direction of where this energy goes, and, instead of releasing it, you redirected it internally to power something positive? What if you could capture and convert this sexual power?

Imagine having the software inside of you to convert that Sexual_Energy.mp3 into Sexual_Alchemy.WAV. What if, in a state of horniness, you could convert your primal urge to release and go from Masturbate.mp3 to Lift_Weights.WAV?

Now you can. All it takes is practicing some good ol' sex magick alchemy.

Sex magick alchemy is for anyone who wants to challenge the roles sex, porn, and masturbation play in their life and doesn't want to conform to norms, instead desiring to shatter those barriers and do what feels right for them.

Sex magick alchemy is a process that one can apply once you become conscious of your sexual energy. When you locate the power of your sexual energy, you can use free will and power to choose how and where this energy gets directed without physical release (the outcome that modern society has programmed us to believe is the only reasonable response to feeling horny). This is a decision a magickal practitioner makes after shaking off the conditioning of society.

Sexual alchemy requires discipline and a commitment to experiment and explore something that might not make sense to most people.

HOW THE BEASTS OF THE MATERIAL WORLD DRAINED ME OF SEX MAGICK POWER

Porn

Have you ever tried to reach a god-high through porn? I have. Porn has been a means for a lot of the young men in my generation to reach their higher selves—the pursuit and attempt to access a spiritual experience while also soothing pain and disappearing as they numb themselves.

Porn was introduced to me as a critical component of the dominance older boys and men wielded over me in social situations, functioning as an assertion of their masculinity and power. I was thirteen years old in 2007, sporting an everyday uniform of the same purple American Apparel sweater as Pete Wentz. I smelled like shoplifted Axe, a hacked Brazzers membership, and weed. I remember being at the house of one of my female friends and her brother saying, "Wanna come see a pic of this pussy in this mag?" I was confused. Was this a rite of passage? Is it the duty of eighteen-year-old boys to indoctrinate young boys on images of porn? Looking back, I guess they wanted to act like cool older brothers, but when I was seventeen, I didn't have that desire to initiate young kids. You just go through with it because there is nothing worse than not having male approval in the suburbs. By the time I was fourteen, I knew the names of more porn stars than US Presidents and senators.

Later, porn became a way for me and my friends to contextualize and understand our tastes during a time of sexual discovery. We would rate girls by the porn stars they looked like. It was a kind of an organizational system. "I would only fuck her because she looks like a porn star, but I wouldn't date her." Or, "Kazems, you could fuck her if you want. If you don't, I will. I hear she fucks like a porn star."

There was a clear split being articulated amongst a lot of the young men I knew, in that porn was teaching us that there were two types of girls: sluts (sexual, pornographic object-women) and girls that were cool enough to date and hang with, pretty and pure, and worth getting to know. It was to the point where we were convinced that certain girls had a porn star look in their faces that datable girls didn't have.

I believe dudes cheat on their girls with escorts or strippers because they are finally satiating that porn fantasy they've been inundated with throughout their teen years, and they can't resist it when they get a chance to materialize it in the physical plane. (Note: Hip-hop videos never illustrate that blue balls at the strip club is neither fun nor glamorous.)

No adult ever explained to us that trying to replicate the sex you see in porn videos can be depressing. Society and social media teach young boys and girls to mimic porn. Why was I surprised when participating in this kind of hardcore sex felt unreal and disconnected, like I was living inside of a screen with zero emotion? The sex I have had in my life that was inspired by porn was selfish and empty. There were times when I felt like a spiritual virgin because I had only ever fucked myself. I was alone in those experiences, thinking only of my own pleasure. Even though there had been another human being in the room, sex just felt like I was at home jerking off to a video on PornHub.

I don't ever remember not having permission to think this way because I have no memory of any adult ever teaching me to respect women or appreciate anything feminine. There was no adult telling me not to objectify women or how to respect them, and there were no men who felt they had any intel on the subject because their only way to bond with me was by bragging about the sex they'd had. I was raised by technology, my friends, and pop culture. These were my parents, my teachers.

The older men I met along the way would explain to me how great it is to be a man and how cool it is to catcall girls or check them out because "they want it," and "they exist for our pleasure." I remember one of my friends in high school posting to Twitter: "She says she has the pussy, so she has the power. Well, I say I got the dick, I got the rape." No one acted offended over this. No one freaked out. No one got suspended. This was normal.

Porn was my sexual education. No one was ever in my ear explaining to me that there wasn't much uniformity between porn and real sex, clarifying that this was acting or Hollywood fantasies designed to keep young boys clicking.

How was I supposed to be smart enough to challenge this when every older man, every rapper, and every male icon I looked up to was somehow reinforcing this power structure and also operating off of this same permission?

I remember my friends talking about watching porn with each other and how gay I thought that was. I didn't feel left out. It was just something I wasn't comfortable doing. They would text me Pornhub links at one in the morning on a school night, and I realized this was a form of bonding that wasn't going to stop. It would be a recurring theme with male friends throughout my life. One time, a female friend of mine was complaining to a group of girls that she saw texts between her boyfriend and his buddy describing a hot girl on the bus in a pornographic manner. She said to me, "Isn't that so gross, Alex?" (Her boyfriend was sending me the same texts with pics he'd taken of the girl.)

This behavior is normalized in today's culture. Men sacredly exchange and post GIFs of the porn and porn stars they are watching while discussing girls they are attracted to on Reddit and bodybuilding message boards. They bond over this collective sexual understanding and loneliness, isolated from the judgment of their wives, girlfriends, mothers, and female friends. Some show their faces; others hide under anonymous ghost accounts, indulging in this carnality, coming together to roast their fantasies over a digital fire.

A loneliness permeates young men. They feel compelled to share their desires because of all this pent-up sexual energy, which makes them feel lost. The only person that can understand them is another man who is filled with the same desire and experiencing the same feelings.

Sometimes I wonder how I'm supposed to feel or react when watching a Pete Davidson interview, and he is telling the male interviewer about the same porn star that I like. I feel awkward. *Is this like a fist bump? Are we bonding?* Or when you listen to a rap song, or read a rapper's Twitter feed, and they are talking about porn you like. Or reading a friend's Twitter, and he is talking about a porn star he likes; and all his buddies respond in support. You even go to a men's website, and almost always, the clickbait is designed around porn and porn stars, and the male writer is talking to the reader like he's engaged in bar talk: "Kill, Fuck, Marry, Kill," encouraging you to objectify women.

I get it. When you find a girl hot, it can be exciting to share your discovery with a homie who agrees with you. I do believe there is something powerful about your sexual tastes and desires being validated and shared by other human beings.

I have had meetings with Hollywood producers and agents in which there always seems to have been an older man in the mix asking what porn I like, the kind of girls I prefer, and bizarre fetish talk that I haven't ever heard elsewhere. This would happen a lot when I was a teenager, and I told older people in the industry when I was shocked and disgusted. All they said was, "Welcome to Hollywood. It's a weird, weird town."

If you don't participate in these forms of bonding, you get called a fag or pussy because coming to terms with your male power and dominance in society is a supposed rite of passage. Rejecting that invitation from other men is considered a kind of violence against the male ego. Part of becoming a man—and being a man—is knowing the power you have in society. Part of that education seems to be agreeing that women are secondary—objects to be acquired and consumed.

I grew up within a generation accessing more porn than any before it. No one was explaining that this endless search for the right clip of the right girl to generate dopamine hits was a complete waste of time, not to mention a waste of magick.

When I came to the realization that porn was an indoctrination and that I had accepted it into my life without thinking about it critically, I felt rage and started to see the harm and violence porn has on the mind and soul. I was angry because I had been taught to think everything I had seen was permissible. I had been blind to the conditioning, unable to separate fantasy from reality.

Now, through the practice of magick, I'm able to see the human being and soul first, before the body. I try to live consciously and not objectify the bodies of others.

The girls I know have told me that having the kind of sex in porn actually hurts, isn't pleasurable, and doesn't do anything to get them to orgasm. Very few get off on the idea of being treated in the ways depicted in so many videos. I know a lot of straight-identifying women who watch lesbian porn because they feel it's calming and nurturing, devoid of the types of violence depicted in so much straight porn. Women aren't just perpetually charged up, waiting around to get laid.

The first time I ever went into a gay bar, I was writing a story for *Dazed Magazine* on Vancouver's drag scene. It was the first time I ever felt myself caught in a man's gaze, being assessed strictly in sexual terms. There was a heaviness to it that completely caught me off guard. I wasn't horny and wasn't thinking about sex. I was just trying to work. I felt grossed out. At that point, it occurred to me that this is how women often feel.

The dehumanization in porn; the fact that it is a fantastical product born from Hollywood boardrooms as a means to monetize a man's instinct to jerk off is disturbing when viewed in the light of day.

Taking back my magick power from porn has been life changing. I was happy to accept that everything I'd been taught about sex was a total fucking lie.

I believe the extreme stimuli you see in porn is what tricks the brain into wanting more. Porn teaches young men to go into a chamber in which they are releasing their procreation power—a potent magickal energy—into the universe to pixelated fertility goddesses on the screen. Porn is a demon of the modern world that holds you captive and steals your energy.

As a culture, and as we enter the next magickal age of pop magick, we need to listen to the voices in the digital communities of young men (NoFap, No PMO) who are talking about the harm they intuitively feel porn is doing to their lives. We should champion them for questioning the consensus. Instead of responding to their psychic pain by saying, "This is weak and typical male appropriation, trying to bring up male issues during a time of radical feminism," we should instead ask, "How can we help you? How can we deliver some compassion and understanding? How can we work together on a solution?" We can feel the same things and reach the same points for different reasons. Our humanity and emotional camaraderie for one another can come through in that understanding rather than measuring our suffering and feeling competitive about it. We need to see each other for the souls we are.

Porn drained me of my energy and time, which effected my goals and magick because at my lower points, I would rather have felt shots of euphoria than alchemize my will and energy into something more powerful and beautiful. I don't watch porn anymore. It's something that I associate with my dead self. I don't see how sacrificing my magickal sexual energy for temporary illusions is productive when it can be channeled into rituals and goals. I'm not letting time—the most precious gift I have been given—be wasted on nothing. Why watch porn when I could be writing, listening to a personal development podcast, working on my magick, or growing my company?

Sex sells because stealing your energy works. When I stopped watching porn, I started to see all the black holes throughout culture that I hadn't noticed when I was inside of it. Porn is everywhere: your YouTube sidebar, Instagram feed, album art on Apple Music and Spotify; song lyrics in your Twitter feed. Porn is as normalized as daily news. When the temptation comes up, you have to ask yourself, "Is it worth giving up my magick to click this? Can I alchemize this into something higher?" It's also most important that you challenge why it is there, and ask yourself: "Why does society always want me to be distracted by sex? Why do corporations want to steal my sexual energy?"

Masturbation

When I realized I had a choice whether to masturbate, I said, "Cya! I'm out" to jerking off. It's messy, makes me feel incomplete, is boring, and gives me a guilt hangover. Ever since Drake said "the realest moment of a man's life is after he cums," jizzing has just never been the same.

I view masturbation as a trait of my dead self, a young-boy who lived off of his automatic impulses. I see him as a child, wanting more and more of this toy I have beneath my belt that can soothe me. Wah! It's not what I associate with modern masculinity. Now, I follow a NoFap lifestyle. (NoFap is a community of young men who abstain from masturbation to deprogram the sexual conditioning they were raised on.) I felt like I had been lied to, that all these things that supposedly made me more masculine were actually making me weaker.

As a magickal practitioner, I am obsessed with freedom, free will and choice, and doing what feels right for me rather than what I've been taught. I believe that when you jerk off compulsively, you are wasting a powerful alchemical state. I also seriously fucking live for the conspiracy theory that spilled semen attracts demons, just because it's hilarious and, honestly, filled with truth. Maybe that's why I've always felt so sad after cumming. "Oh, no! I've summoned a semen demon."

When I get horny or feel an instinct to jerk off, I see it as the perfect opportunity to do sex magick alchemy. Instead of physically "releasing" the sexual energy or sending an embarrassing message to someone on my phone in the "heat of being charged up," I capture that urge, focus it, and force myself to go for a run, do push-ups, lift weights, make a to do-list, or do deep breathing exercises. I follow the alchemy techniques of visualizing the feeling being released from me or visualizing the feeling going through a conversion process wherein I'll see the energy becoming something new and powerful in my mind. This is when I feel the most magickal—when I am taking something and changing the direction of where it goes and forming something new.

The energy I have from sexual desire was not meant to be wasted in Kleenex. It's a power supply to fuel a magickal life. I don't want to waste something that is powerful enough to create life on temporary highs and instant gratification. If anything, there is something that I find rebellious and sexy about myself when I am being disciplined and using my willpower to resist giving in to such a primal urge. It makes me feel like I am in touch with the divine masculine, and I sure as hell don't feel in touch with the divine masculine when I have jizz on my stomach and an iPhone screen in front of me playing a video of two people fucking.

Hookup Apps and Sexting

I believe we are in an Age of Aquarius era of decadence. We live in a culture that is obsessed with sex and wants us to believe everything that we do is connected to the value of sex. It's a lie. It's a trick to get you to spend your sex-magick power and time on artificial highs.

Social media and dating apps have taught us to market ourselves as people to have sex with, rather than people you should get to know: "You want to date someone? You want to fuck someone? Well, put all of your sexual energy towards crafting a persona that will turn you into a commodity that will then determine how sellable you are."

Posting photos of ourselves naked on Instagram and creating porn of ourselves might be seen as a means of self-empowerment to some, but all I see it as is selling your soul to the machine that wants you to be a product rather than a human being. When you are wasting your time on the desire to be seen, wanted, validated, noticed, acknowledged, and liked, you forget that that reward is artificial. You could direct that power into your goals, your career, your own self-validation and happiness, and your own set of standards that don't revolve around what you've been conditioned to believe by our sex-obsessed society.

Someone once said to me: "Isn't that the ultimate goal in our world? To be a commodity that is worth buying?" It isn't in the world of pop magick. When someone asks you for a nude picture, they are asking for a part of your energy. Before you give in and give it to them (The reward/response ends up sounding like something an auto-bot would say in a LiveJasmin chatroom: "Wow, nice cock," "Your ass is amazing." "I love your tits."), ask whether you can simply tell yourself that you have a nice cock, a nice ass, great tits, or whatever makes you feel good about your body. It could be a gap tooth for all I know. These things can't be defined. To believe we need external validation in order to feel seen or whole is wrong. To believe that there isn't a spiritual or psychic cost to exposing ourselves in these digital exchanges is also wrong.

Hookups off apps have always come with the expectation that the sex would be erotic but only ends up as meaningless and empty as the pursuit of being on the app. The idea of sex with strangers can be hot, but the reality is you are sharing your body with someone you don't know, and they could be lying to you about their STI status. You are both using each other in a physical transaction. I can't understand the logic behind putting your body in danger in exchange for instant gratification. I have hooked up before and only felt confused afterwards, like, "How did I end up here?" I don't experience that feeling with people I love or trust.

I can't tell you how many times I've had sex where I felt like I wanted the person to get away from me afterwards because that feeling of horniness, that hunger and lust that needed to be satiated just disappeared, leaving me feeling stupid and asking, "Was this worth it? This person doesn't care about me, I don't care about them, and I don't feel good." It's like discovering you're hungry while you're out and about. You can grab some crappy fast food, or you can delay your gratification and put something nutritious into your body later.

I've been the type of person who has used people on the internet for my own validation. I've even manipulated them into telling me that I am attractive before ghosting them. This is so dark to me because it came from a place of being unable to empathize with the human being on the other end. I would be like, "This person is hot. If she says I'm hot, that means I'm hot." It was all about feeling reassured. I would super like and idealize girls I was attracted to and feel as if I hit the lotto when they liked me back. I regret that I assigned my value to something so superficial.

It's difficult to feel of sexual value in a world where there is always someone hotter a swipe away. We all are just options in the swipe-right culture.

Doesn't all this hedonism make you want to take a nap? How much more sex can you have off of an app? How many narcissistic surface-level dates can you go on, only to dispose of that person when you've found someone better who is liking all your pics?

I wasted too much magickal energy using hookup apps and sexting because none of those things brought me long-term fulfillment. I look at using these apps like gambling but, instead of the chance of getting money, you get temporary validation, fleeting fulfilment, or passing physical release

When I feel the urge to use apps or sext, I channel that sexual energy into being the best version of me, which means working on my career, mental health, and physical health. I realize that bringing a stranger into the mix to validate me is only going to make me spiral. I need to be able to tell *myself* the words that I want to hear from others.

When I meet the right person, it'll happen by natural order.

HOW TO DO SEX MAGICK ALCHEMY

1. Work yourself up into an erotic state. Only you know what gets you sexually charged. Access and meditate on whatever that is.
2. Think of this state, energy, and feeling as something you are going to capture. You can either think of it as going fishing and using a net to capture a fish, or think of it like something

out of Pokémon, where you capture Pokémon in the wild and secure that Pokémon in the Pokéball. You are locking down that feeling.

3. Visualize the feeling having been captured.
4. Now, assign a color to that feeling and imagine it changing into a different color as it alchemizes into a potent new energy.
5. Visualize that power filling up your body to motivate you and drive you.
6. Direct this power outward. This can be directed towards anything from a productive task to a candle magick ritual.

SEX MAGICK ALCHEMY EXAMPLE

Everyday

You see someone hot on the street. You feel filled with sexual desire; you've noticed it.

Options

A. "I have captured this feeling and will change it from red to gold and go to the gym to lift weights."
B. "I am going to look for meaningless sex on my phone, now that I am horny."

Choose option A: "I am going to go to the gym to lift weights."

Ritual Magick

You are alone and sexual feelings are being activated. You feel horny and are filled with sexual desire.

Options

A. "I have captured this feeling. I am changing it from red to gold. I am going to do a candle magick ritual."

B. "I'm going to look for someone in my phone to sext with."

Choose option A: "Light a candle and do a candle magick ritual directing towards a goal."

SEX MAGICK ALCHEMY RITUALS

Charm a picture of yourself on a sex app: Visualize your profile pic and imagine all of your sexual power being amplified by this image, and try to think clearly on what it is that you want this picture to do.

Amplify your sexual aura before going to a party: Visualize the feeling of everyone looking at you, giving you attention in ways that you don't usually get. Visualize yourself being sexually confident in the room and being the one in control of your body and energy. This doesn't mean you are going out to get some, it can just be for your own ego and to feel powerful. You know the feeling when you think you look so hot before you go out, and you are like all Buffalo Bill? *Wow, are you fucking kidding? I'd fuck me.* That's the power of sex magick, and it's coming from you.

Take a hot picture of yourself, and do not post it: You know the feeling when you look into the front view of your iPhone camera and say, "Wow. I look so fucking hot right now. Everyone needs to see me. I am full on Buffalo Bill-I-would-fuck-me mode" and then you post a selfie to your story or grid, ready for your glo-up? What if you took that picture and didn't post it? What if you resisted the pleasure of receiving instant validation from someone in your phone? What if you left an extremely sexy picture of yourself on your camera roll and didn't show anyone, not even your Instagram crush, your sex app crush, or your emotionally unavailable fling? This ritual can help you become less reliant on the sexual validation of others and going into the higher magickal place of alchemy and self-validation. Tell yourself: "I look hot right now. No one can see me and no one can tell me this, but that's ok because I see it. I see myself. I'm worthy and good enough, and I don't need an external supply or source to join in on how hot I feel right now." After you say that, visualize a pink light of self-love filling up your body.

There have been times where I have looked in the mirror, felt sexy to the point of being near tears because of how badly I wanted to share that experience with another person, knowing there were options on my phone just clicks away. But as soon as I started to challenge that and said to myself: "What the fuck? I don't need anyone to validate me," I started feeling more fulfilled and nourished.

SEX MAGICK ALCHEMY EXERCISE:

1. Work yourself into a state of sexual desire by thinking of a sexual experience (real or imagined) that truly aroused you.
2. Harness that energy, and feel it without letting it take you over and drive you to physical release. Think of it as something that just is, and let it exist.
3. Focus on a productive task or artistic endeavor—anything that is a pursuit of your goals or something that is nourishing and makes you happy.

A LIST OF TASKS TO DIRECT SEXUAL ENERGY TOWARDS

- Exercise
- Personal goals
- Art

- Reading
- Dancing
- Ritual

Free will is an important aspect of magick. I am not here to convert you into an abstinent monk or nun. I am here to challenge you; to make you question and interrogate the roles sex, porn, and your sexual energy play in your life. Contemplate the indoctrination of these distractions and question why the Kardashians want you to be so hypnotized by their bodies, why Instagram wants you to commodify yourself. Why do celebrities use sex scandals as a means to get our attention? What instinct in us are they exploiting, and how we can direct that energy into productive behavior?

I am happy with the decisions you make, once you consider the options of sex magick alchemy first. Then you can look back and say, "I'm aware of the other side. I can see how I've been programmed and take control of these things." Thereafter, you can return to the machine with self-awareness, or you can reject the machine altogether. At the very least, you will have the ability to proceed with a better sense of balance that will allow you to retain your magickal power.

HOT TIPS

- You are the only one who gets to define what sex, porn, masturbation, and dating apps mean to you. If you feel indecisive or conflicted, imagine there is no societal pressure and that there has been no social conditioning. What would be the authentic way you relate to these things? Masturbation can be ceremonial for some, and if it's something that you don't feel is depleting you, then continue to indulge.

- In sex magick alchemy, I use something called the "Now what?" technique. You've had a lot of sex with people you're attracted to. Now what? You've watched videos of your favorite porn star or Instagram model. Now what? What is the point of indulging in these pleasures? Are they bringing you genuine pleasure, or are they just distracting you? Is this something you just want right now? Will it have been worth it in a few hours if you give into the temptation? If the answer is no, don't do it, and expend that energy elsewhere.

- If you are trying to abstain from masturbation, try to connect your sexual urges to your hobbies or interests. I have a director friend who grabbed his video camera and went out and shot footage anytime he felt the urge to jerk off. This energy can be alchemized into something even more gratifying than cumming and be released in other ways.

- Imagine your sexual energy existing within a hot spring of magickal energy inside of you. Take responsibility for the use of that pure water. You get to decide how you divert this energy, affect how it can become more noble, and be regenerated as something new and powerful like a handmade crystal.

15

CHARGING A MAGICKAL ITEM

Any item can become magickal. Charging something is a way to bring magick everywhere you go, and remind you of how sacred practicing magick can be, whether you put a necklace up into the full moonlight or direct your energy into a ring for protection. You can absorb the powers of certain moon phases by leaving your item outside on a Full Moon, or draw down the energy yourself.

HOW TO CHARGE A MAGICKAL ITEM

1. Choose an item. In this example, we'll use a ring.
2. Decide if you will charge it with moonlight or with your own energy.

3. If with moonlight, hold the ring up to the moon, and visualize the power of the moon (along with your decided intention) being infused into it.

4. If using your own energy, hold the ring and visualize the power of your intention and energy being directed into it.

5. Now you can begin to use the charged item.

16

THE MAGICK POWER
OF THE MOON PHASES

Have you ever looked up at the sky and drifted into a state of wonder while looking at the full moon? Did you feel that there was something more powerful than your human self, radiating beams of lunar energy and power into the universe?

In magick, the moon is your clock, calendar, map, and mirror. It has functioned as a powerful navigational device for witches, sorcerers, and magickal practitioners across the ages who revered its sacred power and drew upon its powers to advance themselves and modify reality. Timing your magick with the phases of the moon is essential for success. Certain moon phases have more meaning to me than my own birthday.

The moon controls both the ocean and astral tides. Magickal practitioners know how to push and pull this energy. Our magick and psychic abilities change along with each phase of the moon. When you do magick with the moon, it's like creating a private ceremony in which you are wedding the cosmic forces of nature and life. It's pure lunar euphoria.

Lunar light shines on us when we decide to become more conscious of the natural cycles of the earth and allow ourselves to be attuned to the energies emitting from the moon. Our lives become more magickal, and we are reminded that we are more than the mundanities of the material world. The moon transports us to endless dreams, beauty, and boundless possibilities. The moon is a reminder that we are all made of stardust and are children of the cosmos.

The moon is my clock. I see myself in the movements of the moon. I am at my most energetic and productive during the light of the moon. During the dark of the moon, my energy shrinks, and I experience an upheaval of opportunity to make peace with my shadow self. During this time, I have to do the psychological work and alchemy to create space for more light to get in. The moon is my magickal lifeline, and I accredit all of my magickal success to its power.

Each moon phase is a celebration, illuminating the different aspects of the cycles of nature and self: birth (new moon), growth (waxing), maturation (full moon), regeneration (waning). You can learn a great deal about the soul of magick simply by going outside at midnight to look upon a full moon.

A GUIDE TO THE MOON PHASES

New moon: The new moon is the beginning of the lunar cycle. This is the most powerful time to do magick to awaken or invite new opportunities into your life. If you want a new job, new romantic situation, or a fresh start, cast your spells under a new moon. The new moon is a time for growth or expansion. It's also a time for new beginnings. The new moon symbolizes rebirth and begins the waxing cycle. A new moon is a great time to plant magickal seeds and initiate long term plans that you want to come into fruition.

Light of the moon (waxing moon): This is the two weeks following a new moon, when the moon is increasing in visibility and reflecting more light. Light of the moon is a time to bring opportunities towards you and move things forward—to do magick to materialize the results you will to create or increase.

Full Moon: This is the moon is at its full power. You can do magick for anything at this time and create the results you want. This is a time for workings involving major dreams and endless possibilities.

Dark of the moon (waning moon): This is the two weeks when the moon is decreasing and darkening. The dark of the moon is the window between the full moon and the new moon. This is a time for workings involving decreasing anything that does not serve you, shadow-self alchemy, or turning darkness into light. Be careful during this time.

Black moon: When two new moons occur in the same month, the second one is called a black moon. This is a more powerful time to do magick then any other moon phase. It is believed that spells cast under a black moon manifest more quickly.

Blue moon: Every 2.7 years, a full moon appears twice in the same month. The second moon is referred to as a blue moon. This is a time said to be twice as powerful as a typical full moon. It is believed you will receive extravagant results from the magickal workings that you do at this time, and you'll experience extreme magickal activity and vitality.

TRACKING MOON PHASES

Download any moon phase app on your smartphone or go to your local bookstore, metaphysical store, or wherever books are sold online to get a witches' almanac or moon phase calendar to keep track of the daily moon phases. I prefer the annual *Llewellyn's Witches' Datebook.*

MOON BATH RITUAL

There is nothing I love more than a good moon bath. A moon bath is usually taken with herbs, Epsom or Himalayan salts, and whatever oils you feel have magickal properties. You do not need to do a moon bath on the full moon. You can do this during any moon phase. Correspond it with the intention or energy you are feeling from the current cycle. You can do a waxing moon bath to draw in more opportunities or positive energy. You can do a full moon bath to feel your body benefit from what is believed to be a heightened capacity to absorb minerals due to this powerful phase.

I go through a spiritual death during the dark of the moon as I work to transform my darker qualities into the more positive attributes I want when the new moon hits. I bless this new version that becomes formed on the full moon. Then I go through another symbolic death as the moon decreases in light. I do a new moon bath in which I shed the skin of myself, shapeshifting into a snake on the astral plane while visualizing those qualities that do not serve me being sealed away with the current phase. I repeat this bath every moon cycle. Aren't I so extra?

HOW TO DO A MOON BATH RITUAL

1. Set your intention and purpose corresponding with the current moon phase. For example, if the moon is waxing, it could be to bring forward more opportunities, whereas if it's full, it could be for more magick power.
2. Run hot water and sprinkle in magickal herbs, salts, oils, and anything else that you correspond with magick.
3. Submerge your body in the water, and visualize the feeling of your intention soaking your body and filling up your mind, sparking the changes you want to see in yourself and the world.

MOON JOURNALING

Use your Magickal Record to track your emotional, intellectual, and physical reactions to the various moon phases. This journaling will become accumulated data from which you can discern patterns and other evidence about yourself. You can use this information to establish guidelines that work for you going forward and will be helpful in your practice of magick. I have used the data I've collected to become more efficient, productive, and proactive.

DRAWING DOWN THE POWER OF THE MOON

Drawing down the power of the moon is one of the most potent forms of magick that exists. It's simple and dreamy, and can awaken a lot of your magickal abilities by simply connecting to the energies emitting from the moon. Most magickal practitioners draw down during a full moon, but you can do it during any moon phase. In my earliest days of practicing magick, drawing down the power of the moon connected me to something beyond my daily existential pain and transported me to feelings of ecstasy I didn't know were achievable.

HOW TO DRAW DOWN THE POWER OF THE MOON

1. Go outside on a night when the moon is visible.
2. Put your hand up in front of the moon.
3. Visualize the power of the moon entering your palm and then the rest of your body. If necessary, visualize a white beam streaming from the moon directly into your hand.

GUIDE TO THE ASTROLOGICAL MOON TRANSITS

In Magick, we pay attention to the moon moving through each sign of the zodiac, from Aries to Pisces. The moon stays about two and a half days in each sign, influencing the sign it inhabits and causing distinct energies to be emitted that effect our day-to-day lives and impact the various spells we do. By studying the moon's effects on ourselves and our magick, we can learn to forecast and predict how the moon's position within the zodiac will influence the different types of magick we practice.

I encourage every practitioner to do a deeper study of all twelve astrological archetypes so that you can become conscious of the characteristics being unleashed on you and those around you during each transit. However, you don't need to fully understand astrology to incorporate the power of the moon transits. You can do a spell for money on a Taurus moon without needing to know all the archetypal details of Taurus. You simply need to know what sign the moon is in.

I keep track of the moon phases with my Llewellyn datebook so I know what kind of magick and activities to do for the day. The list I've included below will help you understand the traditional correspondences. As you progress along your path, pay attention to recurring feelings, desires, and thoughts, and make note of them in your Magickal Record. I've learned a lot about myself from this practice. I've noticed cool things such as meeting someone on the day of their moon sign, or dreaming about someone I know on the day of their moon sign.

- **Moon in Aries:** A great time to begin things. Things happen fast but pass quickly. People tend to be more combative and dominant. An ideal time for magickal workings involving dominance, attention, and conflict.

- **Moon in Taurus:** Things begun now tend to last a long time. Value will increase over time and will become hard to change.

Brings out an appreciation for aesthetics and sensory experience. An ideal time for magickal workings involving money, abundance, and fertility.

- **Moon in Gemini:** Things begun now can be easily changed by external influences. Time for communication, fun and games, and shortcuts. An ideal time for magickal workings involving communication, duality, and positive attitude.

- **Moon in Cancer:** Stimulates emotional conversations with people. Supports sensitivity, nurturing, and growth. A time for domestic concerns. An ideal time for magickal workings involving alchemy, sensitivity, and nurturing.

- **Moon in Leo:** Draws focus to the self and to general ideas. Connections with others and their emotional needs tend to be on the back burner. An ideal time for magickal workings involving publicity, willpower, and strength.

- **Moon in Virgo:** Favors anything involving details and serving to someone higher-up. A time to focus on daily routine, health, and hygiene. An ideal time for magickal workings involving healing, health, and order.

- **Moon in Libra:** Favors social activities, duality, balance, friendship, and compromise. An ideal time for magickal workings involving intellect, diplomacy, and charming the public.

- **Moon in Scorpio:** Increases awareness of psychic abilities. People tend to become more brooding and secretive. An ideal time for magickal workings involving sex, power, and truth.

- **Moon in Sagittarius:** Draws focus to confidence and travelling. This is a time to be philosophical, adventurous, and athletic. An ideal time for magickal workings involving freedom, travel, and optimism.

- **Moon in Capricorn:** Develops a sturdy structure. Focus on responsibilities, obligations, and traditions. A time to set rules and boundaries. An ideal time for magickal workings involving career success, productivity, and goals.

- **Moon in Aquarius:** Unorthodox energy. Time to break free and make rebellious changes. The focus is on one's freedom and personal individuality. An ideal time for magickal workings involving revolution, innovation, and collaboration.

- **Moon in Pisces:** The focus is on astral work, nostalgia, dreaming, intuition, and psychic feelings. A time to be spiritual and altruistic. An ideal time for magickal workings involving psychic abilities, illusions, and emotion.

If you are interested in going deeper on astrology, try downloading the CoStar app, as it'll teach you about your natal birth chart and the cosmos's influence on your life.

17

CREATING A MAGICKAL RECORD AND DREAM JOURNAL

Book of Shadows, Spell Book, Magick Diary, or whatever you want to call it, a magickal record coupled with a dream record are two of the most powerful documents you can create for yourself as a practitioner. When you study all the variables involved in the rituals that have worked for you, you can record and repeat those variables to achieve more results going forward. A dream journal is essential for documenting the messaging being generated in your unconscious mind. It can help you discern symbols and psychic messages sent from entities with whom you are working. Essentially, it allows you to build a better relationship with your unconscious mind.

I would not have as much success in magick if it wasn't for my discipline in maintaining documents of everything surrounding my magick—especially the moon phases, my mood, and my dreams. It always gives me chills when I look back at the dreams I have journaled, note the moon phase, and learn that I dreamt about someone on the same moon phase they were born under. It's especially enlightening to interpret the magickal symbols and visual language of your dreams.

If you're uncomfortable using a pen and paper, make a Magickal Journal and Dream Record on your phone's notes, and fill it in when you have time. It is essential that this information does not get lost. The data and evidence you stitch together adds significantly to your magickal power.

EXAMPLES FROM MY MAGICKAL RECORD AND DREAM JOURNAL

Date: 3/19/19

- Moon Phase: Scorpio waxing
- Ritual: Green Candle Magick
- Location: Kitchen
- Magick: Scott asked me to do a spell to help him out with getting a new job that will make him happy.
- Emotional State: Passionate, excited, feeling in service of something higher.
- Physical Conditions: Kind of hungry, but whatevs.

- Thoughts: I know this will work. He's going to feel comfortable and happy at his new job. I did the spell on the day of the moon sign he was born under.

- Results: Today is June 13, the moon is in Scorpio waxing, and Scott called to tell me that he is so happy at the new job he started this week. Success! I fucking love magick and when the moon phases come full circle during a result.

Date: 4/29/19

- Moon Phase: Pisces dark moon

- Dream: Me and Aidan were arguing, leaving the front door of a house, and we were going to buy bread. When we got to the bread store (bakery?) I woke up.

- Thoughts: I don't know what the fuck this means. I never dream about anyone. Pisces moons are known to bring upon psychic messages or dreams, but what could bread mean? I've been studying kabbalah lately, and they mention "bread of shame." Does that mean both of us are feeling shame right now? Or could bread mean fertility or abundance? Either way, this is disruptive and annoying to my life because I rarely remember my dreams. I know he joked about doing magick in secret. Is he doing spells on me?

DREAM JOURNAL

Consider the source of your dreams, and realize that none of the internal data you have within you is inane. Your dreams speak to you in a language that only you can only see, hear, and understand.

A dream produces symbols that only you can interpret. The personal symbolism is deeply private.

Trust that your intuition, your subconscious mind, and higher magickal self will give you something that will compensate for what you lack. Sometimes in dreams, our subconscious tries to heal us by holding up a mirror to what we need to change in ourselves.

I believe entities have the power to send us prophetic dreams in which we can emotionally react to something, wake up with that feeling, and alchemize it into magick.

Try to create your own personal list of the repeating symbols you see in your dreams, and assign your own correspondence and meaning to each.

If you have trouble remembering your dreams, affirm to yourself before you fall sleep that you will remember. The best time to recall a dream is when you are awoken by one, especially a nightmare. This is an ideal time to document what you experienced, if only in fragmented language that will make sense to you down the road.

Some magickal practitioners believe that dreaming is a portal to multiple astral planes—that the soul is travelling to different states of being or consciousness. One time, I drank two cups of mugwort (a powerful herb associated with lucid dreaming) on a Pisces full moon to see if I would be able to induce a colorful dream. To my shock, I ended up dreaming of meeting a friend of mine who was born under a Pisces full moon. When I saw her two years later in Los Angeles, it felt exactly like the dream I'd had. I experienced something that cannot be simplified by a concept like déjà vu.

Keep a dream journal near your bed so you cue yourself to get those dreams down before your day begins. Try to remember all the emotions, feelings, details, and anything you saw and heard. This is automatic writing—anything you can remember at the time. It does not have to be perfect or contain complete sentences.

TEMPLATES FOR MAGICKAL RECORD AND DREAM JOURNAL

Magickal Record

- Date:
- Moon Phase:
- Ritual Performed:
- Location:
- Magick:
- Emotional State:
- Physical Conditions:
- Thoughts:
- Results:

Dream Journal

- Date:
- Moon Phase:
- Dream:
- Thoughts:

18

POSITIVE THINKING

Seriously, what is the alternative to positive thinking? Being miserable for the rest of your life? Positive thinking is using your will to think optimistic thoughts to produce practical action and solutions in your life. When you think positive, you figure out ways to make darkness your bitch and take on the world with your innate magickal power.

Positive thinking might be the most powerful form of practical magick and is my favorite type of magickal alchemy. I use it every day when things aren't going as I planned or when I am confronting spiritual trials featuring complex adversities. Positive thinking is simply about changing the direction of your thoughts.

Positive thinking gets a bad rep because a lot of people perceive it as being unrealistic, ignoring the darkness, or being delusional. It's actually quite the opposite of that. Positive thinking is about confronting the darkness and reality—refusing to lie down and die and let the negativity of this world win. It's about figuring out solutions and exhausting all optimistic resources. I believe I'd have nothing that I have in life—including a secure relationship with myself—if it wasn't for positive thinking.

Since some magickal practitioners believe that we must constantly possess thoughts of good health, happiness, and success in order to achieve the life that we want, positive thinking can be seen as a practice of magick.

This can be complicated, because it can create an anxiety of spiritual perfectionism. "Oh, I had the wrong thought. This is why I didn't get that." Try to be chill, and think as positively as you can while being kind to yourself. It's OK to validate your moments of negativity, too, as long as you can avoid falling into the magickal energy-suck traps of nihilism, hedonism, and apathy.

YOU GET TO CHOOSE WHAT TO FOCUS ON

Does the concept of The Law of Attraction stress you out? It can be overwhelming to think positive thoughts all day that emit vibrations and frequencies meant to manifest your dream life. Let me make it easier for you. Think of something right now, like Madonna. See? Now you are thinking of Madonna. In that second, you chose to focus on Madonna. Now, you can have the thought, *I am good enough to follow my dreams*. Or, even better, *I am living my dream life*. From that simple motivation, you can fertilize your garden of thoughts with more positivity to drive you to create the practical actions that you need to produce your dream life.

You have a choice in what thoughts you think. It's up to you to decide what makes you feel good and what style of thinking is constructive and magickal for your own life. You get to choose what you consume. Do you want to hang out with negative people who worry about everything, or do you want to surround yourself with uplifting people who make you stoked on life? Do you want to be worrying about whatever bullshit is being inundated in your brain through Instagram and Twitter, or do you want to be taking the practical steps to achieve your dreams and goals?

When you use positive thinking to choose what you focus on, you start to see that there can be positives to pain, trauma, and daily trials. You can will yourself to see the positivity in negative situations by choosing thoughts that embody triumph, courage, power, and divine will.

ONE OF THE EVENTS IN LIFE WHERE I NEEDED TO THINK POSITIVE

When I was twelve years old, I was told I was going to die. I had been losing weight, couldn't sleep, and was suffering from excruciating pain in my stomach that I can only describe as feeling like a snake slowly hatching out of an egg. When I arrived at the children's hospital, they told me I had Burkitt's lymphoma (non-Hodgkin) and that the cancer was growing at a rapid speed. I could die within a week and needed to start chemotherapy treatment that night. Needless to say, it was a terrifying time and a monumental life event that would shape and breed the addiction, trauma, and psychological pain I'd have to conquer later in life. But at that time, even when all my freedom was taken from me—hooked up to wires, being cut open, waking up with my eyelashes and hair on my pillow, looking down to see incisions all over my body, being ostracized from my peers right before my teen years, and faced with my mortality at a time when I was supposed to feel invincible—I still believed there was hope. I believed I would survive.

Those beliefs started in my mind. In that time of tremendous adversity, the adults around me were in shock because they couldn't understand the strength I had at such a young age. This was how I learned that in your most negative hour, if you have the courage to stay positive and believe something better is coming, you can get through the darkness. Life is full of violent interruptions, but if we see these painful events as being a part of the order of the universe, we can sense the connection to something bigger than ourselves.

You shouldn't subscribe to the idea that being a realist makes you more stoic or powerful. If anything, you lose out on the wonder of life by not being able to test the waters of how things can be if you come from a positive, giving, kind place. This was when I learned life is not a series of chaotic events. I have control over my destiny. I can bring order to chaos with my divine will. Things do happen for a reason. There is order in the universe. You can tune into that, if you please.

HOW TO THINK POSITIVE

Change the negative thought you are having into a positive one. View it from a different angle, and try to see things optimistically. Turn "I can't" into "I can."

Examples of Negative-to-Positive Thinking
Magickal Alchemy

- Negative Thought: I am a failure. I am defined by my past traumas.

- Positive Thought: Life is tough and even tougher on others. I am OK. I have an iPhone, food, and shelter. I am not defined by my past.

- Negative Thought: No one liked my selfie. Does no one care about me? What's wrong with me? Am I not hot? I want attention.

- Positive Thought: I know I am attractive. I am happy with myself. I am neither determined by the approval of others nor controlled by it. I have a lot of people who care about me, and I get a lot of attention.

- Negative Thought: I am never going to be able to be an artist because I don't have the financial security like the rich kids who grew up in Hollywood who can do whatever they want.

- Positive Thought: I am able to work a nine-to-five job and then use my time outside of that to hustle and pursue my creativity and dreams. I believe in myself and what I am capable of. I don't need any other situation than what I have right now to do what I want.

19

PROTECT THE DIVINE FEMME

What are you doing in life if you are not honoring the sacred energies of the divine femme? The divine femme is the expression of anything that our society perceives as femininity: receptivity, emotionality, nurturing, and empathy. I associate divine femininity with sensuality, creation, and intuition. I consider the divine femme as powerful as the rivers and oceans of Earth. Any human being can express and embody the traits of the divine femme, and when someone does, we must honor it.

I believe magick and the divine femme are one because magick is alchemizing the forces of nurturing yourself and others and using your emotions to create something. You can do magick without protecting the divine femme or caring about the divine femme, but that'd be like stealing from nature. If I was stealing all the time, I'd feel guilty.

I try to be a nurturing force for the people in my life who get persecuted for their femininity; those who feel gaslit by society whenever they express something feminine about themselves. Many people feel like they need to hide or destroy their feminine qualities—especially men. These feminine forces can be channeled from any gender. Femininity is equal to masculinity.

When I see feminine demonstrations from men especially, I try to bask in the graces of these expressions.

The misogyny prevalent in today's world is a mission to destroy the divine femme. Modern hatred is deeply rooted in misogyny. Misogyny is a vandalization of the divine femme, which is our Mother Earth. When we objectify and sexualize humans (especially women) by reducing them to their body parts, we play into society's trick to destroy and diminish everything that comes from nature.

It's everyone's right to be as ferociously feminine as they want.

There is inherent shame across all genders for enjoying things that are "girly." Girly should not carry a negative connotation. My magickal self does not abide by these foolish rules! I see femininity as a gift from the goddess, and when I see expressions from any gender, I see them as something of the divine. The goddess particle is activated and at work.

The truth is, our culture is not able to handle the power of the alpha femme. An alpha femme is someone who is assertive, dominant, and strong while also presenting the divine traits of femininity. This can make some humans egos crumble to the core because to be both strong and feminine is to be a threat.

Think of the whiplash caused by a feminine force entering the room. Many immediately feel uncomfortable. I think that unsettling feeling comes from a realization that maybe everything they've been taught is wrong. Maybe, the alpha is the femme. Maybe women are the dominant sex.

I encourage women to be as feminine as they want. There doesn't need to be any Drake in their ear telling them to be humble in sweats and makeup. No one should be afraid of their feminine expressions or the threat they have on men.

I have been taught all my life by many men—straight and gay—to hate women. I have always resisted it. How could I hate such beautiful and powerful beings?

All genders are capable of gorgeous expressions of masculinity and femininity, and this rebellion against tradition will make our species evolve in the Aquarian way we deserve to move forward in.

As a practitioner of magick who is using the forces of nature to advance my will, I feel a responsibility to show appreciation for any demonstrations of divine femininity around me. When we ignore or seek to repress the power of women and the power of femininity, we are lying.

Protecting the divine femme can be exercised in many ways. If you feel inclined to respect Earth—our Mother—by focusing on the environment, that is up to you. We all have different expressions of how we protect the divine femme.

I have always found the highly-charged emotion that emanates from women to be the most beautiful kind of witchcraft. It's a human's right to be as ferociously feminine as one wants, without shame. I view anyone's attempt to regulate another person's femininity as a crime.

You have to listen and trust your instinctual compass. In the same way it feels right for some women to put on lipstick, it feels right for me to put my baseball cap on backwards. It's instinctual. It has nothing to do with performance or conditioning. It's being true to myself, even after I've challenged the conditioning and decided to do what felt right in my soul. If you are cognizant of these constructs of gender norms, if you challenge them and say, "I'm happy with the way I am," that is fine. But try to respect that some people aren't. Some people have been lying to themselves, doing drag in their gender roles. They need to revolt out of those confinements.

I don't believe in imposing anything on anyone. If some people naturally do not feel feminine within, we should not pressure them to be. I think we all deserve to share unity of the divine femme. I do not believe in policing anyone's masculinity or femininity, especially when it's not toxic or harmful to others. I believe in polarity. You shouldn't force yourself to transmute or perform either the masculine or femme if you identify with neither. Maybe you are something that transcends both of those energies. That's futuristic and lit.

I think as long as people are doing what mirrors their authentic souls through their gender expressions, we should not police their choices. I do not believe everything is performative. Certain people exist as mirrors of masculinity or femininity. When we try to modify ourselves in ways that betray our natural selves, that's when we bring forward suffering.

There's a higher reason why we feel so powerful when we activate or let out our more feminine qualities. There is an inherent alpha power in vulnerability, being sensitive, and allowing ourselves to be open to what makes us feel free. It's anti-magick to anathematize your feminine power.

As a society, we need to open ourselves up to understanding what divine feminine energy is. That starts with nurturing the femme in ourselves. If you carry a hate towards the feminine, you carry a hate towards nature.

In magick, we attune ourselves to honor and see the sacredness in femininity, in the expressions of femininity, and our love for those identifying as female and women. These feminine forces can be powerful and channeled from any gender. It's about energy, not gender.

Men who are misogynists set out to try to hold feminine power hostage before it holds them hostage. Weak men despise the true feminine power that exists in all beings because they feel its power and want to compete with it.

The feminine figure, similar to the ancient fertility goddesses, seems to transfix today's society. I understand this because alpha-feminine energy can be like whiplash. Society may view strip clubs as taboo or a contributor to the objectification of women; however, I find it similar to entering a sacred temple of femininity, to honor the women invoking the divinity of the goddess and displaying female power. You can witness the helplessness in men as they are captivated by the power vibrating off of the dancers' bodies. Throwing bills on stage is like kneeling and giving thanks to the power of femininity. This is divine femme magick at work.

HOW A SPELL TO RESTORE THE DIVINE FEMININE LED ME TO TAYLOR SWIFT

Taylor Swift has always been a powerful female force of divine femme energy. To me, she represents that archetype. Swift, in her goddess songs, has told stories about the persecution of being sensitive, feminine, powerful, and all things divine.

When I was in high school, the boys would make jokes like "Swift is the type to poke a hole in the condom," and spin her emotional songs as jokes. This bothered me because I always felt I could relate to her poetic way of experiencing the world. In 2018, I got fed up with seeing how misunderstood her music was by the mainstream press and their erasure of the power of her masterpiece *reputation*. I wrote a piece about her feminism for *Paper Magazine*. I decided to take things into my magickal hands, aka green candle spell time. It was a Cancer waxing moon, and I called upon the divine femme and goddess, saying, "Please send positive healing energy to Taylor Swift, and please get this piece over to her so she can experience a moment of feeling understood amidst all this chaos."

Her fanbase loved it and made it go viral. Many people felt like I was articulating their own feelings about Taylor, and this was a powerful moment for me.

On May 22nd, 2019 (Twenty-two is my magick number!), I attended Taylor Swift's Reputation Stadium Tour in Seattle. On the day of the show, I got an email asking if I'd like to come backstage to say hello. I immediately felt like I was inside of a spell. When I met Taylor, one of the first things she said to me as she hugged me was, "Thank you for making me feel understood."

I was in shock. How did I end up in a room having a conversation with one of my favorite artists of our time? Magick and protecting the divine femme! That's how.

20

YOU ARE THE ILLUMINATI

You there. Yes, you. Come with me. I am going to tell you a secret. You are the illuminati. You simply have to go through the pop magick purification process in order to establish your membership. Magick rules the world, and it's the same kind of magick that you and I can do. That's the truth that few want you to know.

When you become the cult leader of your own illuminati, you become the leader of yourself and make practical decisions to bring order to the chaos around you, thus enabling a divine magickal life. You choose the reality you live in by using your divine will to focus on the kinds of things that bring you nourishment and make you feel aligned with the angelic forces around you.

Being the illuminati requires liberating yourself from all of the energy-sucking vortexes of what I call The Simulation. Like *The Matrix*, The Simulation is the nine-to-five reality you are programmed to accept and participate in—moving forward in a zombified state, blindly consuming from a variety of corporate menus. The Simulation is falling into a job, getting a partner, creating nothing, and then posting to all of your social media accounts about your depression and how you blame the world for your psychic pain. The Simulation synchronizes you to all the various algorithms and keeps you focusing more on memes of Bella Hadid and Kylie Jenner than on yourself, your existential crisis, and all the self-improvement and change you need to accomplish to go from being a reactive person to a proactive person. The Simulation's goal is to destroy your motivation through blind consumption and mindless entertainment. If you choose to stay complicit and comfortable, you risk sacrificing your full potential and power because you sit at home on Reddit reading about Pepe the Frog for fifteen hours when you should be using that time to focus on recording the album you always wanted to record, writing the book you always wanted to write, or filming the movie you always wanted to film.

To be in the illuminati does not require celebrity status, privilege, money, or success. You can be in the illuminati and work at McDonald's. Imagine someone young and broke but full of dreams. They do not self-victimize and know the nine-to-five grind is necessary to facilitate the hustling they do during their free time. This mindset puts them in an optimal position because they can focus their magickal energy on their goals, rituals, and evolution of self. Meanwhile, others spend time in The Simulation, getting drunk at clubs until 6:00 a.m., acting out unresolved pain, and then doing it all again the next night.

I am dedicated to being an illuminati member. I sold my soul to myself and joined the cult of me a while back. I live a disciplined life to protect and preserve myself from distractions. I live by the laws of delayed gratification and silence, and I believe we should only ever present results. I don't let anyone into the behind-the-scenes of my life. I don't have a smartphone. I have an iPod touch with the app store disabled. I have an Instagram account but no access to it. Someone manages it for me, and I have all social media sites blocked. I limit my internet usage, and I question everything The Simulation tries to make me consume. I am only ever focusing on my goals and choosing selectively how I spend my magickal energy. I am not restricted by moving with the crowd, and I live my life how I want to live it. On a side-note, I can confirm that a lot of people in the fashion and music industry practice magick and release things on schedule with the phases of the moon.

Anti-culture is not a subculture that comes from the depths of 4Chan or devil head emojis. Anti-culture starts with you. You are the fucking counterculture. You are the fucking illuminati. When you are the illuminati, you leave The Simulation and dedicate your values to shattering the consensus of the reality you've been born into. You create a new one, a better one—the reality you always deserved. If western civilization is collapsing, we are figuring out how to survive.

22 RULES OF THE POP MAGICK ILLUMINATI

1. We Approve Ourselves

There is no time for comparative thinking or feeling sorry for ourselves over not receiving a digital notification on a dating app or a like on Instagram. We see ourselves and notice ourselves. We don't need anyone else. We look in the mirror every morning with the conviction that we are powerful, valid, and deserving of the kind of lives we want to live. We believe in our worth and don't require external validation. We validate ourselves. We trust a select few for their opinions and constructive criticism (we're only human) but don't go into a panic when a particular person doesn't give us attention. We are not controlled by the highs and lows, the flux of approval from others. We understand everything in life is mutable, and things are there one second, gone the next. When we see someone who appears to be ahead of us in life, we ground ourselves by saying, "I am my only competition." We only focus on becoming better than what we are now.

2. We Choose How We Spend Our Time and Magickal Energy

Time and energy are precious. There is no fucking around when it comes to our magickal energy. We don't spend time on broken, toxic people. We don't overreact and release a valuable alchemical state like rage about world events (which we have no control over) on Twitter just because that's what The Simulation has programmed us to do. We create our own standards and definitions and challenge how the people around us are spending their time. We realize bacchanalian pleasures are always going to be around. When we feel the urge to do something that brings instant gratification/escape but we have work that needs to get done, that activity is functioning only as a distraction. If we delay that gratification to accomplish our goals, that activity will later function as a choice. Focus is more valuable and a potent form of magick.

3. We Choose What We Consume

We don't give a fuck about what meme is on everyone's *Buzzfeed* lips. We understand that the things The Simulation is planting in our brains are to keep us distracted from the things we know we need to focus on. We don't care about the lives of anyone who isn't effecting our immediate reality. We are careful in what we consume, especially regarding gossip, news, and messages from friends who are talking about things we don't give a fuck about. We want to reach a point where we know nothing about anything anyone is talking about, and if the information is neither important, nor pertains to our lives, we instantly reject it. If something doesn't make us feel good, we stop looking at it and replace it with something that does.

4. We Create the Change We Want to See in the World

We don't talk about our ideas, we create and execute them. If we are artists, and we go to the movies and see a film that we don't like, we don't tweet 150 times about it! We go home to write a better script and create a better movie. If we want to see something in the world, we don't wait around for someone else to do it. We do it! We know that the only way to see change in the world is to change ourselves. If we have an issue to champion, we create a well-researched documentary. We educate the masses in a pop way that will entertain them. We infiltrate the media with a virus that challenges the consensus. We surround ourselves with people who want to hack the planet the way that we do, to make our world a better place. We attack our illusions and kill off our inner-cynics. Compete with culture; don't complain about it.

5. We Take Accountability for the Chaos in Our Lives

When chaos is in our lives, we bring order through magick. If we cannot handle the excruciating amount of pain we are in, we search for resources and assistance and spend our time restructuring ourselves to bring order. We are not victims. We are responsible for everything that happens in our lives because our world is built through our reactions to things, and we get a choice in how we react. If we react to chaos with chaos, we produce more chaos. If we choose a different approach, we get magick.

6. We Navigate Reality with Our Own Secret Lexicon

Language is powerful magick. Create a secret lexicon for yourself or any selective members you choose to include in your illuminati. When someone is displaying distractive or toxic traits that I don't want in my life, I call them 1D, meaning one-dimensional. When people display traits I want in my life, I call them 5D, meaning fifth-dimensional. There are tons of words and phrases taken from pop culture that I have reclaimed and speak in secret code to a small group who know the meanings. Bend language to bend yourself to bend reality.

7. We Interrogate and Challenge What the Masses are Doing and Consuming

Everything we have ever been indoctrinated with—from man-made societal constructs to social hierarchies—is challenged. Liberate yourself from the hive-mind mentality and institutionalized ways of thinking. If everyone is going one way, question the direction before deciding on the path that you want to take. If everyone in your friend group is passing around a link of a video that has nothing to do with your life, don't click on it. Challenge the roles porn, sex, social media feeds, and corporate news networks play in your life, and realize there is no law that says you have to abide in consuming anything that does not pertain to your survival or consciousness. If negative behaviors abound around you, react by engaging in self-discipline and establishing boundaries.

8. We Live with Purpose and Intention

We are not nihilistic, apathetic, hedonistic, or anti-spiritual. We understand that there is life beyond the material plane, and we know our souls have a purpose to fulfill whether it's predestined or whether we have to use our divine will to initiate it. We have a connection to something beyond ourselves, whether it's helping others, changing culture, or offering something of value to the world that grounds us beyond the anxieties of modern society.

9. We Are Not Afraid of Power—We *Are* Power

We are not afraid of our full potential and full power. We don't crave power. Instead, we become it by using practical decisions to advance ourselves and our evolution. We are not imprisoned by a better version of ourselves that could exist. We do everything to make that person exist. We do not feel fear about threatening others or losing out on connections with those around us who decide to remain stuck in their cycles and in a state of self-victimization. We realize we deserve a powerful and divine life of magick in which we are fulfilling our goals and being the version of ourselves we want to see in the world.

10. We Practice and Study Magick

Magick is used in daily life. Magick is studied and practiced to create results and change in the natural world. We live a life attuned to the moon phases and to our divine will, and we understand that we can influence reality with the power of how we direct our energy. We study ourselves like a hunter studies prey, and we create our own theories as to why magick works through the evidence and results we create.

11. We Stage Spectacles to Conceal What We Are Doing

We are not brainwashed by aesthetics. We use aesthetics to conceal what we are doing. We create a version of ourselves that represents how we want others to view us. If someone seeks to tarnish our reputations, we regain control of our narratives. People may feel distracted by this version of ourselves. We choose to live a life of privacy and are selective in what we share with the understanding that we are protecting ourselves, making our mistakes behind-the-scenes. We live private, off-camera lives.

12. We Fix Ourselves First

We don't waste our valuable magickal energy trying to fix people who don't want to be fixed or to solve other people's problems. We constantly work on fixing, correcting, and changing what we need to about ourselves to become the kind of people we want to be. We do not allow anyone to take our energy and distract us with their pain and problems that have nothing to do with our lives. We're willing to help people who are willing to receive help, but we can't help people who are unwilling to help themselves.

13. We Are Alchemists

Magickal alchemy is something we practice in our lives. We know we have the power to change things. We recognize and validate our high emotional and motivational states as something that we can direct into a productive, constructive activity or ritual. We are not slaves to our sensitivities or feelings. They are ammo in our arsenal.

14. We Meditate

We meditate daily. We know the power of silence, clearing out our minds, and viewing thoughts as something separate, something to observe. We create the meditation practice we think is best for us by exploring all types of meditation we feel drawn to and doing the ones that work best.

15. We Delay Our Gratification

We know that instant gratification is the ultimate distraction and that there is no way we can evolve into our full power and potential without learning the rules of delaying our gratification. We understand that the fruits of our hard work might not come instantly, but with vision and belief, we can materialize who and what we want to see in the world.

16. We Bring Order to the Chaos

We bring order to the chaos of our lives by taking accountability and responsibility for our roles in our world. Our emotions and events aren't things that just happen to us. Nature's violent life interruptions are viewed as spiritual trials to change and help create the best version of ourselves. This produces more will and strength through our choices in how we react and respond to the things that happen to us, as well as to the things around us.

17. We Are Not Victims

There is no part of our identity that allows us to be a victim. There is no experience that we have gone through that allows us to be a victim. We are warriors and survivors and are not defined by anything that happens to us that is beyond our control. We do not use our trauma for clout. We understand that all pain posted to the internet is viewed as performative and narcissistic. We deal with our pain and traumas in constructive ways and use our will to create resources that can help us, whether it's watching YouTube videos about CBT/DBT or reading trauma-healing books, or going to therapy.

18. We Level Up

We are never at our final forms. We always know we know nothing, that there is more to learn, and that we are humble students of nature, the celestial universe, and ourselves. We challenge ourselves and commit to lead lives of endurance and strength. We understand we will be reborn and die many times, but every time we come back, we are ten times stronger. We treat life like a video game in which we are surviving levels, only to go higher and higher. Our final destination is unknown, but we know during that time we are fulfilling our goals and living the lives we want.

19. We Are Our Only Competition

There is no one else with whom we compete in life but ourselves. We are inspired by the people around us who are further ahead of us, but we only focus on how we can evolve our paths and reach our goals. We know that obsessing over someone else isn't going to do anything for our own lives. We study what our icons have done, and then we do it, maybe even better than them—on our own paths.

20. We Think Positive

We know that positive thinking is how we can survive any trial that nature sends us. We know that, with practical decisions and responses to the conflicts and chaos of the world around us, through positivity we can create order and more bliss.

21. We Do the Opposite of What is Comfortable In Order to Fulfill Our Divine Will

We know that creating something is not comfortable, especially the creation of a better self. We know that there will be times of excruciating pain when we take the step to change ourselves or move further to create the project we always believed we were born to create. When we are met with adversity, we feel it out and realize that what is coming next is going to be worth whatever we are going through now. There is power in doing what you don't feel like doing and becoming better at self-reliance.

22. We Share Our Light with Others, and We Serve Something Beyond the Self

We know we are the only one with the soul we have. We are individuals. We inspire the people around us by being our true selves and sharing the results of the tools we have used to change our lives. We let them know that they can change, too, if they are open to receive and give themselves light. We use the magick of our lives to leave behind something that is beyond ourselves and helps others.

21

PROTECTION RITUALS

A protection ritual is one of the most powerful forms of magick you can give yourself while on your path. It's simple and can be done anywhere. In magick, we use protection rituals when we intuitively feel like we need shielding from a situation or entity.

There have been so many times when protection rituals have saved my life or shielded me during chaotic situations. When I first started practicing and was opening myself to the spirit world, I received psychic attacks in my dreams. As soon as I started using protection spells, I was left alone.

I practice protection spells on every full moon and anytime I feel called to. I fill a cup with salt water and pour the water onto my fingers once I feel the spell is finished. Once completed, I feel barriers of impenetrable, angelic light surrounding me, keeping me safe from any harm or psychic attacks. Protection spells always generate a state of euphoria and relief.

WHY DO A PROTECTION SPELL?

You know when someone tells you something someone else has been saying about you? Protection spell time. I believe in the ancient curse of the evil eye and wearing an evil-eye symbol to ward off this curse. I've seen how powerful this curse can be, and how some people don't even know they are weaving or participating in such a harmful form of magick. I try to be conscious of not talking negatively about others, which is why I wear a red string on my wrist—to remind and ground me. When someone is talking about others to you, or about you, just cut them off by saying, "No, this does not affect my life. I am not listening to this." You might realize ninety percent of your social interaction goes down because most people would rather participate in cursing one another all day through casual conversation or gossip.

What if you are at a party or somewhere public and you get a bad vibe from someone's weird energy. Don't worry, that'll make the spell more powerful. Alchemize it and turn it into light for your own protection.

A protection spell is not just for the physical world. A protection spell can create energies and barriers that keep low-vibe spirits and entities away from you. They are a good reminder that we are more powerful than the spirits and entities who visit us during sleep paralysis, mess with our homes, or disrupt our lives in a multitude of ways.

HOW TO DO A PROTECTION SPELL

1. Fill a bowl with water and add salt. Keep your hands on the bowl during the ritual.
2. Visualize yourself being surrounded by barriers of light. Feel the light protecting you—the energy moving from your toes to your forehead. Think of the feeling of staring at the sun, that blinding light.
3. Visualize that sphere of energy charging the water.
4. If you need to, say, "I am protected from (insert name, situation, entity/spirit, event). I am more powerful."
5. When you are ready to release the energy, pour the water onto your fingers and realize it'll be protecting every ounce of your body.

22

PURIFICATION

Purification can be used before a ritual or just around the house when you are feeling bad vibes. A common way to purify is to light sage and walk around the room to get rid of what you perceive as negative energy or anything else that you need to clear out of your space on an ethereal level. Purification is a great way to mark the beginning of performing something sacred. You can also purify yourself when you perceive there is something off about your own energy by smudging yourself.

You don't have to use purification in a magick ritual, but some swear by it to gain results.

HOW TO PURIFY A ROOM

1. Light an incense or sage of your choice. (You can use smudge sprays or any other purification prop you desire that you consider to be cleansing.)
2. Set your intention. For example, "I am getting rid of all the toxic vibes in this room!"
3. Wave the lit sage, and let the smoke move through the air as you walk slowly around the room.

HOW TO PURIFY YOURSELF

1. Light an incense or sage of your choice.
2. Starting at the top of your body, let the smoke waft around you. Fan it onto your body with your hand or with a low-blowing fan.
3. Inhale a tiny amount of smoke to purify your insides.

23

ENTITIES

I am going to tell you a secret that today's occult world doesn't want you to know. All angels, gods, goddesses, and demons are entities with whom you can collaborate and whose powers you can activate. The concept of advanced magick has guarded this secret in confusing, overly complex how-to manuals, books, and online classes that cost thousands of dollars as a way to make you feel powerless. In pop magick, we give you the straight-up truth that has been hidden from western civilization.

Entities are an immaterial essence that you can create to have a distinct existence in our reality. You can use your conscious will to create a being from ephemeral energy via the thoughts and emotions of your conscious mind combined with your magickal direction. This entity can work with you to manifest your desires.

Entities work through the two magickal practices of evocation and invocation.

An evocation of an entity is to bring forth an energetic force outside of yourself to align and work with, like an angel or demon that personifies the qualities of the entity you intend to call on. For example: I called upon Archangel Raziel, an ancient angel of magick, to assist me with finishing this book. I began to see the number twenty-four everywhere I went, and I received angelic downloads of ideas to my mind that felt of divine intelligence.

An invocation of an entity is to bring forth the qualities, traits, and personification of your idea of an entity from within yourself, such as a fictional character, ancient deity or goddess, or even a pop icon. For example: When I am feeling weak in the midst of a project, I think of the courage and strength Marilyn Manson summoned to finish the album *Antichrist Superstar* during a painful time in his life.

In today's world, it's hot to have a "DIVINE ANGEL 22222 LIGHTWORKER" YouTube or Instagram channel to present your divine psychic powers and connect you to an angel like Archangel Michael, whom you can call on for protection. However, there is no single fixed version of Archangel Michael. We are not all calling on the same Archangel Michael. We are simply calling on the nearest entity to take on the role of Archangel Michael. It's like calling a clinic to find out which doctor has the soonest available appointment.

The only knowledge we have about what entities are capable of comes through their contact with us. Entities may be spirits who were once humans, or they may be energetic matter floating around in the astral plane. Entities may also be facets of ourselves that exist in the depths our mind. Whatever they are, entities love to do drag. They can present themselves as demons, gods, goddesses, angels, faeries, elementals, servitors, or whatever you create them to be when calling upon them. I believe entities are always watching us once we become receptive to them, and they can be playful. Whenever I research demons or something dark, I get a pain in my lower right leg. If I shout out, "I do not fear you!" the pain evaporates.

I have a theory called Entity Cues, which posits that entities synchronize with vibrations and energies in our bodies. They perceive a cue generated by a frequency within us and become free to communicate with us via that wavelength.

Entities are called upon through the emotional or energetic state we choose to feed them. We need to be able to will ourselves into a certain frequency to be able to meet, align, and match with them. If I want to work with an angel, I have to be sure I am in an authentic state of desperation, because angels are said to know when we genuinely need their help. If I want to work with a demon, I have to make sure I am in a state of darkness like fear, because demons are known to love fear.

There is a belief in the world of magick that there is an entity hierarchy. Some people believe there are bad entities like Satan, demons, and servitors, and then there are good entities like gods, goddesses, and angels. I would advise you to not think of things as good and bad but, rather, low and high. I think the darker emotional states we experience can be just as beautiful as the lighter ones.

Entities frighten a lot of practitioners because of their ability to meddle with our lives. Entities can create chaotic events and reality modifications. They have made me fall to the ground into out-of-body experiences in the middle of the day, dragged me around the house, sent me repeating numbers as a means to let me know I am on the right path, and modified my reality in order to send divine messages. I work with entities daily, and I call upon them during rituals and send them to create the results I want out of my spell, because I believe they play a huge role in my magick.

Entities can visit us in dreams to warn us about things, meddle with us during sleep paralysis, send us messages through repeating numbers or any other strange occurrences. Some witches say they've had sex with entities and have even gone on dinner dates with them through astral projection. Entities will communicate with you and present themselves to you and, through magick, help you achieve what you want.

When working on this book, there were days when I would be reading one of my favorite magick books for reference. If I moved the book near a speaker, the music would glitch out, and when I moved the book away, the music would return to normal. This was either an angelic presence or spirit who was present and working with me.

Once you summon and start to fuck with the forces beyond us, you have to accept responsibility for the unseen, unknown, and unpredictable. There is no guaranteed direction in which the astral tides will sway you. If you open yourself up to supernatural magick, expect the unexplainable. If you are reading an e-book you found on Google at three in the morning that tells you to call on a chaotic demon, and you do the evocation, causing your life to *coincidentally* shatter in chaos several weeks later, that's on you. There's no book that's going to tell you how to undo a sudden drug addiction after selling your soul to a demonic entity. This is real-life shit.

Building a relationship with the unknown astral otherworld is neither a positive or negative thing. For me, it's how I can feel safe in my life. When I know I am being watched over by celestial bodies of energy, it makes daily life a more pleasant experience. I feel they understand the truth of my character, and they can see my intention more than most human beings. Entities are here to intervene when we need them, but we shouldn't rely on them. We should prove ourselves to be the powerful entities we want to see in the world and to handle our trials ourselves.

Entities are neither good nor bad; it's about your intention and what you choose to create in your reality, if you even want their assistance. We don't play safe in magick; we play smart. All we know is that when we call up the astral worlds, there is always an entity that will answer.

ENTITY CREATION

Why follow a dogmatic book that tells you to call on ancient gods or goddesses, demons, or angels when you can create your own holy guardian angel, assign qualities and powers to it, and work with it in your life? I've created angel entities who have appeared in my life as ghosts. A long-distance friend on Instagram can be like an angel from the astral plane because you are communicating with them on a non-physical level. You can feel the energies we communicate and send to one another through the ether.

Entity creation is saying, "Fuck off" to the manuals and guides to contact ancient goddess, gods, demons, and angels. It is taking things into our own magickal hands. If there is no angel or demon you identify with—if the entity you need to exist to assist you with your life or individual situation doesn't exist in any of the books in the occult section at your local book store—create and will your own into existence. A true guardian angel is yours.

How to Create an Entity

1. Call out to the astral plane and say, "I am ready to receive communication from magickal entities I will to work with and create. I am open to the spirit world for all your divine guidance to bend reality in accordance with my divine will."
2. Decide on the identity of the entity you will create. It could be an elemental spirit, a god, a demon, a goddess, a mermaid, or an angel. For example: "Luzuroph" will be an angel entity.
3. Decide on the specific goals or purpose of your entity and what you would like your entity to assist you with. For example: The purpose of my angel Luzuroph is to protect me from unrequited love and abandonment.
4. Decide what energetic state of emotion it'll feed on to exist. For example: Luzuroph will feed on self-love, optimism, and perseverance.
5. Write out a description of your entity. For example: Name: Luzuroph. Type: Angel. Powers: Protection from unrequited love and abandonment. Correspondences: Water, Masculinity. Energetic Food: Optimism, perseverance, self-love.
6. Call on your entity. Close your eyes and feel your body creating the energetic food. Watch your hands thrum with energy to let you know your entity has arrived and is with you.

7. Call on the entity for assistance. Ask the entity to communicate with you.

8. Thank the entity by saying, "I am happy to have made contact with you."

9. Begin to work with this entity in magickal ritual as well as your daily life.

ENTITY ENERGY FOOD LIST

All entities survive by feeding off of emotional states and vibrations. To evoke an entity's presence, you need to be in a state in which it'll be able to match with you. You might already be in that state when you choose to call upon an entity. The state for angels to feed off of could be a desperation for help or joy. Demons are known to feed off of fear, lust, hate, and pain.

- Emotions = energy
- Emotional states = food for entities
- Angels: desperation for help, bliss, euphoria, kindness
- Demons: fear, pain, lust, hate

SIGNS OF ENTITY CONTACT

Have you ever encountered repeating numbers during the day? You check your receipt, and there is the number twenty-four. Anytime you check your phone, you see twenty-four. Anytime you check the clock, you see twenty-four. You turn on the TV, and it was last left on channel twenty-four. This may be an entity trying to make contact with you. Entities can modify your reality, and if you pay close enough attention to the magickal repetitions and reoccurrences all around us, you can listen to the messages they are trying to communicate. It could be a deceased relative or an entity who is trying to get your attention. Below are some of the ways in which you may experience the presence of an entity.

- Repeating numbers
- Newfound abilities
- Things appearing out of nowhere
- Items moved around

MY MAGICK NIGHT WITH AN ANGEL

An intense magickal experience happened to me in the year 2019. It was the night of the Libra full moon. I had experienced something bizarre while listening to Lana Del Rey and doing my laundry earlier that day. A song came up from an album I had never heard of, by an artist I had never heard of. I was confused and just thought it was someone on my apartment floor bumping me off my JBL FLIP by connecting their phone to it by accident. Later in the day, I opened a magickal book I had never opened before to a page about evoking an entity that would take on the role of the Kabbalistic angel of Raziel. I called on him and asked him to assist me in magick and the journey through this book. I came home after a session at my outpatient rehab and opened my Spotify to put on some Madonna, only to find another album in my recently played list that I had never heard before. The first song was called "Magic," with the length of 2:11! 2:11 is my spirit guide number, and the number twenty-two is a number that is always being sent to me from the otherworlds. I started to cry because of the chills and confusion. No one knows my Spotify password. This was angelic activity—reality being bent right in front of my very eyes. I listened to the music, and it felt like angels were making my whole body hum. This was one of my most profound and powerful experiences.

Immediately, I felt drawn to google "communication with Raziel" and found more connections and alignments with my life situation. The next day, my friend was in a metaphysical store where an angel card deck was out, and when I called, she told me she had just pulled a Raziel card from the deck. When you contact entities, they will come to you and send you signs. Pay attention to the messages. I wear my Raziel talisman to feel protected and have had more powerful magick then ever from working with him. Coincidences are not real, but magick is.

24

BLACK MAGICK

Magick doesn't have a color. That's a myth meant to restrict and instill fear. Magick is only about intention. Good, pure, bad, and evil are subjective constructs produced by society. Only you have the colors to fill in, and you get to decide what those words mean to you.

It's your free will and human right to do whatever you want to do with magick. I am no magick moralist as long as you take responsibility for the chaos you could create with destructive and harmful intentions.

How you use the tools and power of magick is up to you. We can't dictate one's intention, let alone their will. If you choose to go down a magickal path that is seductive to you because it's Satanism, the left hand path, or black magick, challenge that instinct, and think twice before you devote yourself to what could be a journey through darkness.

It's a terrible waste of magickal energy to banish, bind, curse, or hex someone when you could be using that force to advance yourself in the world in a positive fashion.

FREE WILL

There is no right or wrong way to utilize magick. You can choose to follow the guidance of dogmatic religion or spiritual practices that involve magick. The same magick that is used to help someone is the same magick that can be used to harm someone. You decide the role free will plays in your magickal practice.

25

MAGICKAL AESTHETICS

The power of aesthetics rules our world. We are inundated with calculated images and symbols that are crafted with specific intentions to generate likes or persuade us to purchase things.

Everyone wants an identity, and having a story to tell yourself about yourself can be fun because it gives you a sense of belonging, but not all practitioners of magick look like we were extras in nostalgic nineties movies like *The Craft*. Some of us practice in private because it's an area of control. For us, that is sacred. There are practitioners of magick who conceal themselves within everyday crowds. That businessman you saw in a suit on the street an hour ago might be full of magickal knowledge. Magick used to be practiced in private, but now it is very much out in the open.

When you practice magick, you start to correspond and associate certain things as magickal. You do not need to have an altar, pentagram necklace, or talisman with runes on it. Anything can become magickal. Did you ever have a lucky bracelet as a kid? That lucky bracelet could be viewed as charged with magick.

When I first started practicing magick, I fully identified with being a witch. It made sense to me because I had finally accessed the part of me that I always wanted. Becoming conscious of the power of nature, moon cycles, lighting candles, and communicating with the spirit world gave me a sense of identity. Those magickal feelings that were awakened have never gone away, and I can think back to certain incenses I've found in metaphysical stores or the feeling of discovering a new stone that I felt drawn to with great bliss. I used to wear a pentagram ring everywhere I went, and sometimes I would turn it upside down so that I wouldn't be asked questions. I was silent about magick, and I wanted to see if other practitioners could pick up on my aura. An older Scorpio friend who had stopped practicing once told me, "You are dripping in the spells you've done." I enjoy that closeted practitioners can feel that I am open to the spirit world.

A lot of celebrity friends in Hollywood who practice magick in private become shocked at how transparent I am and how I talk about my rituals with them in daylight. "Don't you want more for yourself?" A lot of people feel that being silent about their magick is an aesthetic in itself, as well as a way to protect themselves and to create more powerful results.

Today, a lot of people like to post about the magick they are doing and create social media accounts based on their magickal identities. I think this is great to create community, but do not feel pressured to participate. Some people view these people as frauds or fake, but I do think if you are posting about magick and witchcraft and you aren't practicing, you are doing yourself a disservice.

Aesthetics are one aspect of magick, but practicing magick is one hundred percent more important than anything else. It's a disservice to the practice and power of magick to simply embrace it as a fashion statement.

As practitioners of magick, we are all allowed to be excited by the aesthetics we associate with magick, but there is no wrong or right way. When I see candles, I feel that beautiful ecstasy of being under the light of a full moon, while someone else might get that feeling from seeing a poppet.

What you consider to be beautiful, and the associations and correspondences that create your own magickal aesthetic, can only come from you. You can't learn it from a book. You are the only divine version of you. I can't tell you what shards of your soul are mirrored back to you or what reflects your own nature.

HOW TO BUILD YOUR MAGICKAL AESTHETIC

Go to a metaphysical store (online or offline), and see what you are drawn to. Look around. Test the waters. Do you feel connected to pentagrams or statues of angels? Maybe you are more drawn to the aesthetics of Hoodoo or La Santeria. Listen to your soul's compass, and do what feels right for you. Embrace the aesthetic that you feel connected to the most or invent your own.

HOW TO USE THE POWER OF MAGICKAL AESTHETICS

Charge your Instagram posts with intention. If you use Instagram and are wearing or have something sacred and magickal, make sure you charge it with an intention. Or maybe even hold up your phone screen to the lunar light and visualize the combined power of your intention charging the post. Your intention could be, "This selfie of me holding a ritual candle will make anyone who looks at it feel self-love."

Create the magickal person you want to be and see in the world. If you want to take magickal aesthetics up a notch, create an image based on your magickal practice and knowledge. Ask yourself: "What would I want to look like as a magickal practitioner? Am I wearing all black? Crystal bracelets? Archangel talismans?" Think of your idea of yourself as a magickal practitioner, and bring that to fruition through your fashion and pic choices. Invoke the magickal entity within you, and decide your intention behind the aesthetics.

Create the magickal environment you want to be in. Nothing is better than spicing up your environment with a little magick. I love to have incense going, candles lit, potions and herbs I've made sprayed in the air, angel stones, and statues of gods and goddesses representing the equal divinity of masculinity and femininity. Creating a magickal environment doesn't mean making a witch's altar and having a panic attack about getting the right athame. It means adding whatever you consider to be magickal to your space.

26

SEXUALITY AND GENDER SHAPESHIFTING

When you start practicing magick, you open yourself up to the spirit world. Don't be surprised if you begin to perceive people as souls more than humans. When you start to view people on a soul level, you may find yourself more attracted to their inner qualities versus their external attributes. You may even find yourself seeing beyond gender. When you view humans as magickal souls, the confinements of the physical body begin to shatter. At that point, endless potential for love with another soul beyond the physical can arise.

I have heard stories of people who start to experiment with their gender or sexual identity once they begin to view the human body as a temporary shell for their astral being. Once you remove the constructs of what society has taught us, opportunities to explore and shapeshift present themselves.

I believe we must let all humans be who they are—to let them love and express themselves however they want as long as they are not harming others or themselves. I don't judge anyone for their sexuality or gender identity. Whether you identify as a straight male but like to make out with dudes when you are drunk or you are a bi girl who genuinely enjoys sex and romance with both males and females, all expressions of sexuality are welcomed. In pop magick, we view everyone's souls on their own paths and journeys. We let people walk unencumbered on their paths, and we don't persecute anyone.

You don't need to identify as LGBTQA+ or know anything about queer culture to experiment with the same sex. I encourage everyone practicing magick to explore their sexual and romantic fantasies, whether it be experimenting with your gender identity, accessing your more feminine or masculine qualities, exploring what it means to be non-binary, or trying sex with the same gender. No one owes anyone an explanation about their sexuality.

I know a lot of queer people who do not identify as LGBTQA+ because they believe the fluidity of their sexuality cannot be confined by labels or letters. I've met jock-type guys who enjoy cross-dressing while their girlfriends dominate them. I've met straight-identifying guys who dabble with men every once in a while with their girlfriends in threesomes. I've met hyper-feminine women who do not fit any of the stereotypes of a lesbian but identify as one. I know many trans women who have only dated masculine, cisgender men. Everyone can be many things or one thing. Everything is acceptable.

Unfortunately, we can't learn about sexuality or queer people through the media because much of the representation is slanted, extreme, and burdened by stereotypes. We can only learn about the fluidity of gender and sexuality by believing and listening to the stories of the people around us. We should never invalidate someone's sexual or romantic feelings because of our own pre-conceived notions when that person takes the chance to be honest with us about what they are going through. Before people are their sexual or gender identity, they are a soul. Be free.

HOW I USED MAGICK TO PLANT A POP VIRUS

I have known Diplo since I was sixteen, when I started to write about new artists for the blog of his label Mad Decent. I've always wanted to collaborate on something with him because of his open-mindedness and because he always operates from a mindset of wanting to excite or shock mainstream audiences. Even though it took nearly a decade for me to get to a point where we could collaborate, it happened at the perfect, divine time in the universe.

Despite being a champion of diversity, Diplo is largely perceived through a lens of hyper-masculinity as a true alpha male. When I began a guest turn as Features Editor for the inaugural edition of *King Kong Garçon*, I knew that I needed to do something shocking with him. I've always been fascinated by the idea of corrupting pop culture iconography and filtering it into a warped, confusing reality. This was the chance I'd finally earned from hustling and networking all those years, to be behind the scenes, shaping a major fashion magazine's cover that would be seen worldwide. It was the perfect opportunity to communicate something magick to the masses.

I called up NABIL, a music video director in Hollywood and friend of Diplo's who I wanted to handle the cover shoot.

"We are burning the suit!" I told him. "He's always in that goddamn fucking suit."

"Yeah," he said. "Fuck the suit."

I sent NABIL my treatment to dress Diplo in drag and he immediately got on board. I texted Diplo about the plan and he responded, "k yeh, let's do it."

Diplo has always been someone who stands for unconventional thinking and imagery. It's a big reason why he pushes so hard to infiltrate the mainstream with obscure sound. He's a big believer in innovating, and introducing audiences to sounds they would never imagine loving. He subverts genres and expectations.

For some reason, I got a sick thrill out of being able to shock his frat-bro audience, scarring their brains with something that looks like it came from a different planet. The last thing I wanted was a boring GQ portrait. I wanted to use my air time to create something weird and pop that I wanted to see in the world. I wanted to shatter the public's masculine image of Diplo. Diplo intuitively understood the vision as a "weird flex" as he believes masculinity can sometimes be a prison for men.

Under the next full moon, I took a green candle out to do a specific-outcome spell in which I visualized holding the magazine in my hand, seeing the image on the cover and experiencing the feeling of elation it would bring. Additionally, I added an abstract outcome twist to the spell in which I intended for there to be a big surprise as the end result. I didn't know what it would be. I just felt intuitively that it was coming.

It took nearly five months to line everything up for the shoot. There were many trials. There was a point where I thought everything would fall apart, but I held onto the hope and magick that this was going to manifest. I still believed I'd be able to hold that cover at some point.

The shoot happened in August 2018. When I finally received the raw images from NABIL, the team at King Kong was shocked at how much we exceeded our own expectations and it became one of our favorite covers of the season.

In the beginning of November 2018, just as the magazine was about to hit newsstands, Diplo posted the cover image on his Instagram, cleverly tagging me with a credit for "hair." The press loved that he was appearing in drag. I felt like I was living in a pop fantasy. That was only the beginning, however. I had completely forgotten that I asked for something special from the universe during my ritual to manifest this cover. Later, when I was least expecting it, I received a text from a friend.

"Alex… Are you breathing? Did you see this? Are you okay?"

"What are you talking about?" I asked.

"Madonna. She commented on your Diplo cover."

"WHAT? NO. THERE IS NO WAY. MADONNA? NO!"

I received the screenshot and there it was, Madonna commenting from her official account, a simple, beautiful "Wow."

I texted the screenshot to Diplo and he responded with a row of heart emojis. In that moment, I felt a true convergence of life and magick. Madonna, a pioneer of unconventional pop imagery and one of my favorite artists had just endorsed my vision. I went to the mirror, looked at myself, rubbed water on my face, and said, "I just impressed Madonna. Something from inside of my mind that would not have existed without my will to create it was just transmitted to Madonna, and she is impressed. Magick is real."

27

MEDITATION

I am sorry, but there are no excuses! If you have time to share histrionic Instagram posts of your life, tweet out all your feelings, go into black holes on YouTube watching two hours of beauty bloggers, and watch whatever Netflix Original has just come out, you have time to meditate.

I'm so bored of listening to everyone's excuses for why they can't meditate:

"I don't know how to do it!"
"I can't shut my mind off."
"I need my edge. I like being chaotic and on the go."
"There are too many different types."

This is all nonsense. If you want to start practicing magick for real, meditation is a master key and portal to unlimited self-knowledge. It can be used to alleviate, uncover, and shatter psychological traumas. Meditation can also bring you peace, mindfulness, and awareness of your emotions, feelings, and environment.

We are living in such a powerful Age of Aquarius right now—one where you can download some British dude teaching you how to do mindful breathing in a click. You can will it into existence simply by downloading an app. Why ignore a resource that has the ability to change your life?

Meditation can assist you in magick because it teaches you how to be disciplined and focused. Magickal results require mental power. Meditation has helped my magick because it taught me how to clear my mind. As you now know, achieving a zero-mind state is essential during ritual and after you cast out your energy. Meditation can be a diving board to jump into the pools of your soul.

Meditation has taught me to observe my feelings simply as flashes in my body and to view my thoughts as speeding cars passing by. They are just happening. I don't need to believe in all of them. I now view my mind as a machine that is generating all manner of output—artistic ideas, paranoid or cognitive distortions, anxiety, decisions. I get to choose what to focus on. I used to climb inside of the temporal reality every thought inflicted, always worrying, suffering, and stressing 24/7. I was a maniac and not a fun person to be around.

HOW DAVID LYNCH CHANGED MY LIFE

Last Summer, I briefly met David Lynch at a private event in LA. When I spoke to him, I told him that he taught me that "internal bliss and peace comes from within since I had been practicing

TM." The reality glitch is that I hadn't yet practiced Transcendental Meditation, but I wanted to will it into existence so that I would be able to re-order the events of reality. I knew back then that I was thanking him for something I fully believed was going to manifest itself.

Later, a friend in Hollywood suggested that I reach out to Bob Roth at The David Lynch Foundation to help me with my addiction and trauma issues. This was at a point in my life where I had just checked into an outpatient rehab and was ready to take that leap into the light. I reached out to Bob Roth (the man who taught Oprah how to do TM) with the intention and belief that this was going to unfold a new beginning for my life. He got me set up and into a four-day course at my local TM Center. Those four days changed my life forever—everything from the group meditations, the knowledge from my wonderful TM teacher, and the sacred elements that I associate so deeply in my heart with the enlightenment.

TM is my favorite form of meditation. I meditate for twenty minutes twice a day—once in the morning and once in the afternoon. I haven't missed a day yet. The best part about TM is that it's mine. It's coming from me. The light I access belongs to me, and I am the one taking myself there.

Before TM, life felt like being trapped inside of a snow globe that was being shaken every second of the day. Life after TM feels like breaking the glass that held me in the snow globe. TM is the ecstasy, bliss, and happiness that I had been searching for my whole life. No matter what trials present themselves, I can always return to the simple truth that I hold the keys and password to access the light within me. No one can take this away from me.

Now I can go back in time and see the magick had begun the second I spoke to David Lynch. I was thanking him for something that I believed was going to manifest before it did. Do you see how magick operates on its own timing, and that magick is not about the order of events in reality but the results we intend to create with our divine will?

Higher consciousness is not a ladder to climb or a destination. It's something you have inside of you already. For more info on TM or to find your local center, go to tm.org.

HOW TO MEDITATE

I am not a meditation teacher, and I am not certified to tell you how to meditate, but what I can suggest is that you download apps like Breathe, Headspace, or Calm. You can also watch some guided magickal meditation videos on YouTube. All of these are great, but nothing beats going to a local TM Center and doing the four-day course.

28

MAGICK TO HELP OTHERS AND THE WORLD AROUND YOU

Most people have received a text from someone saying, "Please send positive vibes" to them or someone else. Sending positive energy to others is everyday practical magick that we all participate in at some point.

Using magick to help others is one of the most satisfying aspects of being a practitioner. When someone is asking for your support or help, it can be a bit banal to simply text them back saying, "Sending positivity." Instead, you can do something productive with that state of desire. Doing magick for and with others can create intimacy by fertilizing an already existing bond. Some practitioners do not believe in using magick to help others and only believe in performing rituals for and on yourself. However, some of the most successful magick I've done has been with the intention to help others. I've seen my magickal influence help friends get jobs, advance their careers, and help them heal during difficult times. Mostly, I did the magick with their permission, but sometimes without, which is a bit of a risk. In those cases, I told them after, and they thanked me. It should be your practice to always ask permission.

Living in these tumultuous times, inundated with the injustices and corruptions of the world, we exist in a constant state of stress, thus producing a lot of highly emotional states. Being triggered by world events along with being triggered by how the people around us are reacting to these events can cultivate a powerful magickal state. Why be powerless—a victim shouting into the void—when you can do a ritual to try to influence things and bring order to chaos?

I believe in the unlimited possibilities of magick so, yeah, when I meet witches who tell me they can influence the weather, I don't even blink!

In today's culture, we've seen a resurgence of the group-magick technique that gained fame in the occult world in 1940, when a group of British witches organized a group-spell against Hitler to protect Britain from a Nazi invasion. To this day, this ceremony is cited as evidence by some as to why Hitler never crossed over. This technique can be seen today in everything from young witches joining powers to hex the Stanford rapist, Brock Turner; to the out-of-the-broom-closet, all-American pop artist Lana Del Rey, who helped organize a worldwide group spell on Donald Trump. It's also common for young witches to go on websites like Reddit or becomealivinggod.com and ask magickal practitioners to assist them with their intention.

Voting is a type of group-magick. There is an intention set to vote for a specific-end result, during which multiple people gather together to direct their intention at the polls.

It's safe to say when we magickal practitioners combine our energies together, we can influence world events, help others, and use our energy to shape the world we want to live in. Revolution begins in the mind. It starts as a thought, and there's a power to the energies of thoughts. Words can become action, and actions cause change.

I did a spell once for Rose McGowan to be cleared of the drug charge she faced in 2018. It felt like a set-up to disarm her of her power. Rose and I were communicating a lot at this time. She had a tremendous amount of empathy for the spiritual trials I have faced, just as I did for the slaughter of trauma she has gone through. I did the ritual on a Sagittarius full moon (both of our moon signs). When I saw the headline a few months later that the charges had been dropped, I couldn't help but wonder if my ritual had been influential. Either way, I thanked the universe and the divine femme goddess for this triumph.

When we do magick for others or world events, we can never trace back whether what we did influenced the results. Who cares? The ritual worked!

HOW TO DO MAGICK TO HELP OTHERS

1. When someone asks for help, determine what their intention is. If it's "please send good vibes that I am confident in my job interview," you know the intention is that this person wants to feel confident.
2. Visualize and feel the passion, belief, and support you have for this person.
3. Build the energy in your body, and then, when you are ready, visualize the scenario in which they are accomplishing the intended goal they want.
4. Direct that belief and energy towards them, then release.

HOW TO SEND POSITIVE VIBES TO SOMEONE

Visualize the person you intend to help, and feel your energy filling up their body with white light. When you feel it's ready to be sent—a feeling that you're about to burst—release it!

A LIST OF THINGS TO CONSIDER WHEN DOING MAGICK FOR OTHERS AND WORLD EVENTS

1. When you do magick for someone, consider how well you know the person. If it's someone you don't know well and they end up not being in your life very long, are you going to be OK with your magick continuing to work? We don't know how long magickal boosts and charms last.
2. Ask yourself whether this is a productive way to use your magickal energy. If you feel too drained or exhausted to give

your energy away, you can direct the energy that they want to yourself and self-preserve.

3. If your rituals for others or the world work, it's best to keep it to yourself. When we talk about our magick, we can weaken it. Silence is power.

4. Get consent. Don't sit around lighting candles for everyone in your life for whom you feel empathy. That's a quick way to drain your power and a waste of your energy.

5. Some magickal practitioners believe that doing magick for others is an interference and can affect the natural order of events in their life, which can have karmic consequences. If this makes you uncomfortable, you can say to an entity before the ritual: "If [insert name here] is willing to receive this energy, I am sending it. If not, please send this energy back to me to alchemize and further my divine will."

29

MAGICK MISINFORMATION

Never treat anything you read or hear about magick as fact. Base everything on your own practice, evidence, and theories. Create the magickal system you want to use in the world if those that exist don't work or feel right for you.

You are no different than Aleister Crowley, Doreen Valiente, or Anton LaVey. You are on the same earth that all the most famous occultists lived on, utilizing the same energies they had access to. Do not fall prey to false worship. You have access to unlimited occult knowledge. You do not need to adhere to any hierarchy. You can become as powerful, if not more powerful, than those you admire or idolize.

Create your own path, and do not feed into people in the occult community claiming to be living-gods with more power than you. Develop your own personal relationship with magick. You are not doing magick to join any cult other than the cult of you. Do not trust people who claim they can teach you powers or are "the human reincarnation" of a god, goddess, angel, or other entity.

The main difference between science and magick is that a scientific theory needs to be replicated multiple times in order to be proven true. Magick cannot be replicated nor can your experiences. That is power.

30

MAGICK SAVED MY LIFE

"I'm not meant for this world," was something I believed from an early age. If people knew the details of my life, it would be easy for most to blame the series of traumatic events that spurred my depression and self-destructive tendencies, but I think it's more beautiful to see this pain as a seed—the beginnings of a spiritual trial that was set upon me to be conquered.

My deep-rooted feelings of isolation and disconnection created some dark pursuits where I ended up confused and lost, travelling through worlds I never wanted anything to do with, all the while maintaining a profound belief that there was something better for me—if I could just survive.

I spent years in chaos, bonding with nihilism, hedonism, and apathy. I had convinced myself that there was nothing past the human self, that there was nothing but suffering. I went so far as making a pact with myself to end my life before I turned twenty-five.

Something I never understood about myself was my ability to do things to the point of no return. I was driven by a desire to disappear—to obliterate. Everything I did was an attempt at pain management. I just wanted to soothe my mind through any type of euphoria I could manufacture.

I regret the hours I wasted, the magickal energy I spent, and the years I lost to false pursuits, always coming up empty while promising myself, "This is the last time!" The more powerful, glamorous, and successful I would appear to others in my career, behind the scenes, I was fading out as the sickest demon I'd ever encountered. I could not continue to operate off of my unconscious programming, reliving the same toxic cycles and not being able to see that I was the common factor to all of the chaos in my life.

I felt like I had two options: suicide or continuing to live like a victim. I didn't like either, so I decided to take things into my own hands by checking into rehab and beginning the process of recovery. I established a goal to defeat all the negative patterns that prevented life from being magickal. I reached into my subconscious, that monstrous slime, to overcome the enemies within me. I began to purify my mind, along with my body.

I was spiritually wounded, going through life not knowing what was wrong with me. When I was awakened and realized I could choose the role I would play in the video game of my life, I felt the most human. When I discovered what it was in my psyche that had been the root source of chaos and suffering and set it free, life began anew. Everything that happened before that moment of discovery was a spiritual trial preparing me for the freedom to become myself. I resolved to no longer be held hostage by trauma, anxiety, and fear. I would no longer chase illusions. It wasn't until I put my hand in my chest and pulled out the charcoal trauma-chip that was powering me, held it up to the sun, and melted it down into an angelic elixir that I accessed the light within me. That's the moment I took my life back and brought order to the chaos.

Looking back, living a life enslaved to the beast of the material world created confusion and chaos. I believe the material world is what suffering and hell is. We have to survive the trials of this life to be able to receive the light in our lives.

Now, I'm able to view pain as an opportunity. I never blame anyone for making me feel anything, because no one on this earth can make me feel anything unless I give them permission to. I have found that when I assigned blame to other people, it has just been a great way to avoid acknowledging the truth that I am responsible for my life, and the more we run from the truth, the more it'll manifest in chaotic existential pain. If I feel rejected, I can create something, explore it, tell a story about it, and create an image about it. I respond with magickal alchemy.

Every day is like being reborn again, because this is the first time I've gotten to experience life as the person I fought to become. When I think back on life before recovery, it's like watching home movies of a stranger. Now I'm in control, and I've recovered who I was meant to be.

There is no more time left to feel misunderstood. You can't hand over the colors of your world to another person. I stopped caring about my reputation. Angels are the only ones who know the truth about me. I believe that I am part of something that has already happened before. I believe all the events in the universe were aligned before I got here, and it is my soul's duty to survive any trial that is put in front of me—to level up.

It's not about the pain or even the subject of the trials I've seen so far, it's about the fact that I survived them, and I will continue to. When life has another violent interruption for me, I will still be connected to the power of magick and remind myself that I am protected by my angels and nature.

Magick helped me see myself for who I truly am. It's turned chaos into light and turned a wounded boy into a magickal man.

OUTRO

You can change your world through magick. Keep practicing; keep trying. Try to do a magickal ritual every full moon. Keep exploring until you find what is comfortable and right for you. You will get stronger and better over time. Give yourself the gift of believing in magick and seeing magick all around you everywhere, every day.

The treasure chest of tools to do magick is within you. You can access them whenever you are ready. Now go out in the world, and start to practice magick. The world needs your results, theories, and discoveries.

Remember: To bend reality, you must first bend yourself.

Enjoy the ride, and safe travels.

ACKNOWLEDGMENTS

I never graduated high school, but I guess this must be what it feels like to write your yearbook statement or whatever?!

Thank you to my beautiful mother, father, sister, my little brother Romeo, and all of my cousins, aunts, uncles, and family friends for being supportive of my dreams, even when nothing made sense to any of you.

I want to thank the incredible Jacob Hoye, my loyal and powerful editor, who is the only reason that this is even happening right now, by divine synchronicity. Thank you for all of your time, hard work, and for passing down your mastery. I want to thank everyone at Permuted Press and Simon & Schuster for turning my dreams into a reality.

I want to thank J.S. Aurelius for turning my sketches on hotel stationery into a vision far beyond what I could have known or imagined.

I want to thank Daouda Leonard for your unconditional support and consulting over the years and for believing in me even when I didn't know what the future had in store for me.

I want to thank Gabe, who has been the best assistant a man could ask for.

I want to thank Kelly Cutrone for the life-changing call where you inspired me to get my shit together during one of the lowest points of my life. You stoked the flames that needed to be lit for this book to materialize.

I want to thank all of the people that I have inspired who have taken the time to write me over the years. You guys keep me going.

I want to thank anyone who took a chance on me in the beginning of my career. I know that I have always been a risk; to have believed in my potential and ideas is something made of bravery, and I acknowledge that.

I want to thank Marilyn Manson, Bret Easton Ellis, Ariel Pink, Diplo, Justin Raisen, Camille Paglia, Banks, Rose McGowan, Nancy Jo Sales, Brooks Brown, Kembra Pfahler, Kristin Prim, Shirley Manson, Charlotte Free, and Floria Sigismondi for inspiring me over the years. Thank you for providing me with words of artistic camaraderie and understanding in ways that no one else could.

I want to thank Taylor Swift for teaching me how malleable reality can be, that everything can happen if you will yourself to dream big enough, and for making me aware of all the magick that enters your heart when you reclaim and display your pain by putting your experience into words.

I want to thank The David Lynch Foundation for changing my life. Thank you to David Lynch, Bob Roth, and Erik Martin. Thank you to my TM teacher, Anne, to whom I am forever in debt for all that she has done for me. I never would have been able to finish this book without the tools of TM.

ACKNOWLEDGMENTS

I want to thank my incredible Equinox trainer, Richard, for teaching me the power of momentum and pushing yourself. The lessons of persistence I've learned from you are so powerful.

I want to thank the team of therapists who helped me with my recovery these past five years, giving me the strength to leave behind my past life, past self, and addictions. You taught me that when you want to heal, you can, and when you want to change your life, you will.

During the conception of this book, I realized that the trials of the last few years have brought me to some dangerous places while carrying around a lot of misplaced love.

I want to acknowledge all of the dark people that I met on my journey and my travels on both the material and astral plane for all of the lessons that I needed to learn when I didn't know who I completely was. I am so grateful to leave your worlds and lives behind me.

I want to thank the people who I expected would show up but never did for motivating me and teaching me the power of alchemizing the shattering heartbreak of rejection into my divine will. You taught me that I had to lose everything to become the man I needed to become.

I want to thank all of the people I created fantasy bonds with who never actually cared for me. Thank you for teaching me to take accountability and to bring order to the chaos of my life.

I am so grateful to have been magnetized towards a tumultuous series of events that would cause suffering; these trials opened the doors to self-knowing and strength.

I want to thank all of my haters! Thank you to all the gatekeepers in the fashion and music industries who tried to block me from accomplishing my dreams out of fear. What's good!?!

I want to thank all of the beautiful souls that I have encountered who ever took the time to strike up a conversation with me about magick. Thank you for your curiosity, your openness, willingness, and wonder for something more. This one's for you. I thought about our conversations during every word I wrote.

I want to thank nature, my angels, and TLOTC for your protection. 22.

This is a hard one for me, but something that I have had to accept about growing up is all of the appreciation and flammable love that I have, all of the details, feelings, passion, and highs that I experienced with every friend, family member, and enemy that I have known. Every single heartbeat that I have about another person cannot be quantified or shared. As high as I get off of feeling something for someone, no one will ever absolutely understand how much I feel and appreciate. I just hope that those I choose to tell that I love in this life really know that I do, and that behind that word is a colorful experience, even if they do not understand it. Maybe it's too sacred to express in words.

There are too many special people that I've encountered in my life, and no one will ever be forgotten. I can't decide on your value, because you are all too precious. You all deserve to be on this list if you've ever loved me, hurt me, hated me, wronged me, known me, wondered about me, spent more than an hour of your time with me, or even grew up with me in my lifetime. If you think that you deserve to be acknowledged by me and you are reading this, then this is your acknowledgement. I am so grateful for you.

ACKNOWLEDGMENTS

There is someone who has been on my mind for the past six months. You know who you are, and if I haven't thanked you enough already, I will say it again. Thank you for the time that we've had together due to the strange magickal events that brought us into each other's lives. Because of you, I'll never be the same.

I want to thank all of the beautiful people that I haven't met yet who will be a part of my future.

I want to thank Mirwais for the incredible conversations that brought excitement, passion, and understanding during insular times while writing this book.

I want to thank Madonna for teaching me through your lyrics how to bring a voice of spirituality to our world in a practical, accessible way.

I want to thank anyone who gifts this book and shares it with their friends and any reader who discovers something about themselves.

I hope I can make at least one person in this world feel less alone; that'll be my greatest life accomplishment.

ABOUT THE AUTHOR

Alex Kazemi is a pop artist, creative director, and author. His work has been featured on Apple Music, *Dazed*, *i-D*, *Playboy*, *Resident Advisor*, *King Kong*, *V Magazine*, *Paper*, and *Oyster*, among others. He served as Features Editor for the inaugural edition of *King Kong Garçon*. He lives in Vancouver.